The

Tabernacle

Living in Power through Abiding Prayer

TIMOTHY C. DUNLAP

Copyright © 2014 by Timothy C. Dunlap

All rights reserved. No part of this book may be reproduced or transmitted in any form or by any means, electronic or mechanical, including photocopying, recording, or by any information storage and retrieval system, without permission in writing from the publisher.

ISBN: 978-0-578-07464-1

ISBN:978-0-578-13423-9 (ebook)

Unless otherwise marked, Scripture quotations are taken from the New King James Version. Copyright © 1982 by Thomas Nelson, Inc. Used by permission. All rights reserved.

Scripture quotations marked NIV are taken from the Holy Bible, NEW INTERNATIONAL VERSION®. Copyright © 1973, 1978, 1984 by Biblica, Inc. All rights reserved worldwide. Used by permission.

Scripture quotations marked KJV are taken from the King James Version of the Bible.

Printed in the United States of America

First printing—January 2011
Second printing—June 2014

WWW.TabernacleHome.com

Cover Design: N2 MOTION PRODUCTIONS
N2Motion.com | 1.866.N2M.8800
Interior design and typeset: Katherine Lloyd, www.thedeskonline.com

This book is dedicated to the "Private Prayer" teachers whose Biblical instruction continues to inspire their practitioners. Such faithful dedication to this solitary discipline requires a work like, "The Tabernacle," to pay tribute to their efforts. Oneness in God, through Christ Jesus, should be a simple message, but it is not. It is a hard task, so we join the effort in this lifelong struggle to encourage Christians everywhere, especially as the heart grows weary, to *hallow God's name.

---

* *Hallow* See Addendum 6

WITH APPRECIATION

My gratitude goes out to Richard Pierce of Research Optics for his graphic depictions of the tabernacle elements. His many hours and faithful desire to replicate these forms based upon his interpretation of the original Bible text was illuminating.

My deepest thanks to Daniel Davis, Paul Hawley, and Ron Widman editorial consultants, for their encouragement and support throughout the rewriting process. Their patience, dedication and guidance through the subtle nuances of our English language during the dismantling and reforming of the manuscript, and book, have been profoundly appreciated. I truly am blessed of God to have found such skilled craftsmen with reliable Biblical understanding. Their challenging questions regarding the esoteric nature of some spiritual content while holding to the defense of the faith were most helpful. My hope and confidence is that the readers of the following material will be the beneficiaries of an orderly and systematic feast of the eyes because of their labor.

Contents

OVERVIEW 9
INTRODUCTION 13
1. HOLY GOD 21
2. *HOLY* CHRIST 29
3. MENO 45
4. ABIDING ONENESS 59
5. GOLDEN LAMPSTAND 71
6. THE TABERNACLE 89
7. TEMPLE OR TABERNACLE 97
8. BRAZEN ALTAR 103
9. ARK OF THE COVENANT 119
10. DISCIPLES PRAYER 127
11. OUR 137
12. OUR FATHER 145
13. THE WATCH 155

14. APPLICATION 181
15. PROPHECY OR PREACHING 197
16. THE NAME............................... 223
17. SUMMATION.................................

Addendums
  1 ORTHODOX JEWS 235
  2 APOSTASY 242
  3 OTHER CONSIDERATIONS................. 249
  4 TO DO / NOT TO DO 257
  5 PROPHECY.............................. 262
  6 HALLOW................................ 264
  7 ANOINTING 266

BIBLIOGRAPHY............................. 269

NOTES 271

Overview

This book is intended to help the church body find its true source of strength by learning to pray. Many opinions have complicated this subject, and the author seeks to simplify its understanding and apply the Bible to adoration—worshiping God, and supplication—praying for others.

Prayer has a divine purpose, which could simply be stated as conversation with the divine One. God has established its plan, players, and its supernatural parts. It cannot be completely comprehended in this realm, yet it is as widely accepted as it is neglected. Prayer is personal and only sometimes public. Most of us incorrectly assume its usefulness is determined by the negative influences affecting our lives.

That said, too many in Christendom do not get it, do not do it, and too often do not believe in it. We write about it because we are commanded to love God and to love our neighbors. These are relational issues requiring communication or prayer! Simply said, all prayer fits into two general categories: *love God* (worship, adoration) and *love your neighbor* (supplication and intersession). This book concerns the former, the "first things," or loving God.

Our subject, loving God first, is simply prayer between

creature and Creator. Though the primary purpose of prayer is loving God, the impact of prayer upon one's life and subsequently upon the world is without measure.

The intended reader of this book is the Christian. Unless one is born again, prayer is a waste of time. Without Christ within and God's Spirit of Holiness within and upon one's life, God's supernatural mechanisms for prayer lie dormant. Because prayer is communication, and communication is relational, one's relationship with the divine One must meet the standard God Himself has established in the Bible.

Though the target audience of this book is the church body, the primary focus is the prophetic community. This book is not a teaching tool as much as it is a prophetic declaration useful for teaching. Also included are encouragement, warnings, and announcements of judgment for the leading of others in loving what God loves. God loves spending time with His creatures; after all, He created us for fellowship (See addendum 5).

This book deals with prayer in its most practical biblical application for the reader. There will not be found in these pages the traditional manufactured rituals that may distance the creature from an energetic relationship with his Creator. This material is practical, and understanding its application is to recognize the perfect design of the Trinity for the Holy Spirit's teachings of the Word of God. Prayer is not private, but it is done in private! The church needs to know that there is much work to be done in the area of getting alone with God in Christ Jesus.

God's plan for prayer has been illustrated in the Hebrew tabernacle. This was a bloody instrument for purifying the Jewish people, God's first choice of the ones chosen to come before

Him. In addition to the Jew, the Gentile nations, everyone not a Jew, are told that they too may come before God. An Old Testament prophet wrote of Gentiles,

> Even them I will bring to My holy mountain, and make them joyful in My house of prayer. Their burnt offerings and sacrifices will be accepted on My altar; "For my house will be called a house of prayer for all nations" (Isaiah 56:6-7).

In Moses' day, blood sacrifice made things holy and provided people with an acceptable access to God. This was done by slaughtering innocent, spotless animals, and sprinkling their blood upon lamps, tables, altars, and priests within the tabernacle, or the temple of God. This was the law found in the first few books of the Bible including the judicial book of Leviticus.

Today, blood sacrifice continues to cleanse the children of God, but it is Jesus Christ's blood that does so. Part of the reason God gave mankind a tabernacle and a temple was to show us how to become clean to worship Him. Another reason God chose to have all of those animals slaughtered by Levitical priests was to show us how important His Son was to Him.

Today, instead of an endless stream of slathered animals, Jesus Christ is that sacrifice. His blood may very well be sealed within each born again—born from above-Christian while cleansing them from within. God has heard the ones truly asking for this sealing to be placed within them whether they understand the dynamics of this process or not, and by God's power He seals Christ within the heart of those trusting in His Son.

Later in this book, we will learn how the tabernacle continues to function with blood, how prayer is illustrated in its various forms and purposes to draw you close to God through the ministry of the interior Christ.

The esoteric nature of the following material has the appearance of going against popular prayer practices. Therefore it is necessary to appeal to the authority of the Holy Scripture. That process of returning to scripture is what this book attempts to accomplish.

Because God's ways are perfect and His teachings are timeless, timing is of great importance in the matter of reintroducing these truths to the world. Whenever we come to the time and place God is choosing to open our understanding to His will, His sheep know His voice, and they come "in and out" and find pasture.

Introduction

The single most important truth found within the pages of the Bible is the fact that "Christ Jesus lives within you." This truth is not spelled out in any one line or paragraph in Bible scripture as much as it is the primary component of an established system of parts for saving lost people.

The New Testament does not record the words of Jesus explaining the vicarious atoning properties of His own blood within believers. Nor will you find references to His perfect, sinless life qualifying His blood to be used within His followers for expiation, and propitiation—all terms we will learn about later in the book. What we do find in scripture conforms itself to the rules of scripture. Such rules are numerous and they include some of these fundamentals:

- Scripture does not contradict itself.
- At least two references can be found in the text confirming statements, principles, and ideas with each other,
- Context must always be used to interpret scripture,
- and often there are things to be understood out of scripture immediately, things veiled by the use of parables, poetry, symbolic form and apocalyptic literature,

- and there are things not to be understood until the time God has deemed for their unfolding.

The tabernacle and temple concept seems to be one of these shadowy applications of an instrument we have had in observation for hundreds of years while it's true purposes lay hidden.

What do we really know about such deep things of God and His creation? Answer: not half of what we will one day know! Consider this scripture, "…we see in a mirror, dimly… (1 Corinthians 13:12)," and "…we are children of God; and it has not yet been revealed what we shall be (1 John 3:2)." Therefore, with the help of these rules of scripture applied to the deep things of God, we can rely on the Bible to teach us the essential truths as well as the non-essentials.

Christians believe that Christ Jesus the Lord is in them, an essential belief. Do Christians believe that it is Jesus Christ's actual blood in some configuration that may include the cellular structures from His actual body, a nonessential belief, there abiding within us? Before we make these introductions that point us into the great and deep ocean of these spiritual possibilities discussed in depth later in the book, let us briefly state this truth of which we all should know—that God's Spirit is within us.

The Christian who reads the Bible knows that the Bible teaches an indwelling Holy Spirit within Christians. This is an essential belief. While this may be true, there has not been much scientific, or Biblical teaching upon the working dynamics of this spiritual reality.

On the other hand, If we believe that we are actual sacrificial temples employing blood sacrifice once resident in the body of

Jesus, should this be classified as a non-essential belief? Further, our observation of tabernacle/temple sacrifice always included the element of shed blood, an essential component of the Judeo-Christian belief system. Lev. 17:11b "...for it is the blood that makes atonement for the soul..." Gladly, the Holy Spirit understands God's design far better than do we, so it is toward Him we turn for help in sorting these things out.

The Bible teaches us that we are not saved by an idea, not saved by an event in history, though factual. To be clear, WE ARE SAVED BY THE BLOOD OF JESUS CHRIST, an essential belief. Read your Bible! This is what we understand from observing its truth, in the volumes of its pages proclaiming the power of blood supernaturally applied to the life of the believer. The spiritual temple of God, which we are, may require admittance into the essential systems of our faith.

> "Do you not know that you are the temple of God and that the Spirit of God dwells in you?" (1 Corinthians 3:16).

Paul reminds us, in the above verse, that not only are we the temples of the "Holy Spirit of God," but that we are also the temples of "*God*." This reference to "temple of *God*" may be telling Bible learners that Christ Jesus is within us and that Jesus is *God*.

I believe that the apostle John and the apostle Paul observed much more than they were empowered to communicate in their writings to the church. I will go into much more detail about these two apostles later in this book. It seems that God's plan, as the evidence shows, did not include speaking plainly of Christ and

His throne room actually within a believers body. "Your throne shall be established forever," and "God will give Him the throne of His father David." (See 2 Samuel 7:12-16, Luke 1:31-33).

Truly Jesus was fully man having DNA properties from the line of David, Mary's ancestral forefather. Jesus Christ also was fully God, pre-existent and eternal, and all knowing (John 1:1-3, 18:4).

So let us review what we shall find in the claims of the Bible concerning Jesus Christ the man, and Christ Jesus—the one spilled out in blood upon the ground in expiation and atonement for our sin. To be clear, "Jesus," and "Christ Jesus" are one and the same. How? I do not know!

Below, is a short list of truth we will be covering in depth and illustration later in the various chapters of this book, but for now observe:

- Paul understands *Christ*, or *Christ Jesus* mysteriously within you well enough not to suggest the phrase Jesus Christ (the man) lives in you. His word construction is very important (one might consider exploring, "en Christo," a word study theme found in many Bible commentaries).
- There appears to be many layers of spiritual truth beneath the common understanding of the book of 1st. John. Remember that John was taken up and is an eyewitness from having been to the place called heaven.
- The abiding Christ is sealed, by the Holy Spirits power and authority, within a knowable place within the human body illustrated in *types* by the tabernacle and the temple.
- Christ abides where He is sealed and does not coalesce with human flesh or blood. By illustration, a foreign

embassy exists in a state separate from its host nation.
- From out of the heart, Christ may literally speak life through us and into our world by the Holy Spirit.
- Jesus walked upon water in authority over His creation and the indwelling Christ sustains Himself independently in a place the Bible calls "the heart."
- Jesus' flesh did not see corruption (Psalm 16:10, Acts 2:31), "for the life of all flesh is its blood" (Leviticus 17:14b). Jesus' blood by definition is incorruptible.

The Tabernacle/Temple, a *type* for the human body, may be the strongest evidence that Christ Jesus, by atoning blood, may reside within Christians. This evidence speaks throughout the entire Old Testament context in fact, that there is no remission of sin without the shedding of blood. The "Lamb of God," an *antitype*, speaks of the Old Testament "*type*" of sacrifice upon the altar as an atonement for sin.

What purpose does a temple serve without the sacrifice and the offering of blood? Christ Jesus was anticipated by God to be sealed into each Christian by the Holy Spirit. He is then most useful in various places within His temples "not made with hands," that we as believers—these temples would be witnesses to the love of God to a dying world. Our bodies are the temples of God, as seen in the Old Testament *type*, therefore, we require atoning blood as a propitiation for our sin.

The circumstantial evidence of Christ within each of us will be found in more detail as you venture through the pages of this book. That is not a bad thing as much as it is a veiled thing as we said by the use of parables, poetry and apocalyptic literature.

Historically, the tabernacle was the instrument God gave

the Jews for access to Himself. It cleaned up the Jewish sinner allowing for communicating to them His love. God's love also included a wonderful land of opportunity, a place called Israel for their settlement. Also, with the tabernacle's many components, it did things for the Jew's God required while He brought them to this Promised Land.

As we examine together the major components of the tabernacle, we shall see what God was saying to the Jewish people of that day—the tabernacle's interpretation. Because this tabernacle was to be taken to a Promised Land to become a temple, we shall examine what the temple means to us today—its application.

The tabernacle trained the ancient Jewish people to love God first. Then this instrument would gain them access to the Promised Land and there they would find peace with God and build Him a permanent place for worship.

What does this book attempt to say about the modern temple, and what does it really do? The answer to this question is amazingly simple, for the temple does just about the same thing that the ancient priests did in ancient times in their temple with the exception of the following things.

1. Today's priest operating within God's temple is actually you! Remember our scripture, "Do you not know that you are the temple of God." Your soul or spirit in humanness abides in the temple of God. Therefore, the operation of this temple is performed by the everlasting soul—which soul is the animating you within your body (the temple).
2. The components found in the tabernacle are not physical objects, they are spiritual offices coordi-

nated by your spirit and the Holy Spirit inside of your temple.
3. The Holy of Holies, a place within the temple, is actually a space above the Ark of the covenant. This knowable place has great spiritual significance which we will discuss later, though rather obvious within God's plan.
4. Blood was and still is used for the remission of sin (cleansing offenses). The big difference is that God anticipated the death of His only Son, allowing for the spilling out of that precious blood—once and for all, for cleansing and private access to Himself.
5. Blood remains primary to temple operations, water (brazen laver) and oil (menorah lamp) symbolize the work of the Holy Spirit. Loving God and loving your neighbor are made possible by blood but actuated in power by the Holy Spirit.
6. Animal sacrifice continued for fifteen hundred years and changed people very little, while Christ died once for all and mankind will never be the same.

Nevertheless I tell you the truth. It is to your advantage that I go away; for if I do not go away, the Helper will not come to you; but if I depart, I will send Him to you (John 16:7).

In large measure, the reasons Christ could not send the Holy Spirit within believers, prior to the time He stated this verse, were two-fold. He had not presented Himself as payment for the sin of the world, and also, at that time, He had not shed His blood to apply to human tabernacles. Until His blood flowed out, His work was incomplete to save people and satisfy the just requirement for sin against God that gains us access to the power of God, by His Holy Spirit.

Finally, our priest within this temple, which gains us access to God, must have something to say to God. What is more welcome to God than His very own Son's words spiritually spoken from out of our hearts? The Lord's prayer—commonly referred to as the disciple's prayer is most dear to the Father. I know you will enjoy the truth from the Bible and the thoughts that await you in those subsequent chapters upon this prayer, so enough said upon that topic.

I believe the ones who will look up unto God and hallow His name in persistent exercise will be the ones who will be trusted with His next set of battle plans. I am hopeful that includes you and your family and friends in the midst of revival.

Take up the challenges within this book and lift up your face to God, He has been waiting for you in a way you have got to experience.

> The Lord makes poor and makes rich;
> He brings low and lifts up.
> He raises the poor from the dust
> And lifts the beggar from the ash heap,
> To set them among princes
> And make them inherit the throne of glory.
> For the pillars of the earth are the Lord's,
> And He has set the world upon them
> (1 Samuel 2:7–8).

1

HOLY GOD

God loves us! Because we are told He is our creator, it makes sense that God loves us. That is a wonderful fact, but the problem we face with this truth is that we are not able to love God! That is, we are not able to love God unless we have met the requirement in the Bible for loving a Holy God: Leviticus 19:2: "You shall be holy, for I the Lord your God am holy," Are you Holy or perfect? Matthew 5:48 says "Be perfect as your Father in heaven is perfect." The Bible reminds us that we must be Holy, "As He who called you is Holy, be Holy in all your conduct" (1 Peter 1:15).

John 3:16 tells us, "For God so loved the world" that He gave His only Son. Do you care that He sacrificed His only Son that you would be free to love Him? Did you know that God wants to make your life joyous, fun, and filled with purpose through His Son Jesus? But He cannot do so unless, like Him, you are Holy! Once we begin to understand that we can be Holy to love God, this will free us to want to love Him more and more each day in deeper ways.

God wants to be near you, and He wants you to learn what the Bible says about holiness. He wants to hear from you, planning to meet with you often through a method we know as prayer. As you read on, you will learn that prayer is an *antitype*, a depiction of a spiritual reality portrayed for us in a *type* of structure for relating to God. That *type* is called the tabernacle.

A Holy God often speaks His spiritual messages to the world through a visible system called *types* and *antitypes*. Here is what the nineteenth-century Jewish expert Alfred Edersheim says about *types* in his classic work, The Temple—Its Ministry and Services: "The sacrifices of the Old Testament were symbolical and (typical). An outward observance without any real inward meaning is only a ceremony. But a rite which has a present spiritual meaning is a symbol; and besides, it also points to a future reality, conveying at the same time, by anticipation, the blessing that is yet to appear, it is a *type*." The *type* is often called a shadow in scripture. This thing or person precedes and prefigures a greater thing or person, and is called an antitype.

When we learn that praying is doing for us today what the tabernacle did for the Hebrews thousands of years ago, our view of prayer changes. Prayer of this kind always empowers us, for it brings us near to God. It brought sinful men and women before a Holy God by a blood sacrifice. Today, proximity to God is made possible by the blood of Christ which is key to a powerful Christian life. The tabernacle reveals God's present design of a working system of spiritual processes utilizing the blood of Jesus that satisfies His Holy requirement for oneness with Him.

The prayer you will learn about in the pages that follow will not be the kind of praying that people whisper or say under their breath. Private prayer is not for helping loved ones, supporting them, or protecting others. This sort of prayer is not to be streamed out of your thought life, like a set of instructions for a Holy God to follow.

It is prayer from your heart to God. It is the prayer by which you show love to God. In the Old Testament of the Bible, it was called a peace offering, a burnt offering as well as sin and trespass offerings.

Instead of praying with your mind alone, you will learn to pray both with your mind and out of your heart. You will learn that Christians have another heart. In other words, this new heart originated as a *type* found in a component of the tabernacle called the brazen altar. It also corresponds with a place in your lower abdomen, an antitype. You will learn to pray the words of Jesus from your heart in a way the Bible defines as abiding in oneness. Again, personal fellowship with God is private prayer, and it is done in private.

As a holy person, you will learn to stand in power before God with your hands raised or sometimes at your sides. You will find value in the many incidents in Scripture that hint at prayer posture and marvel at this spiritual phenomenon at work while your prayer is happening.

You may be surprised to learn that you can know the habitation of God while you pray to Him! It is not that such a notion is mysterious, but it is mysterious that such a biblical truth could be so simple. The facts revealed in this view of the tabernacle and its furnishings may transform contemporary Christian thought and instantly clarify many so-called contradictions and problematic portions of Bible text.

Consider the various items of furniture in the tabernacle. These furnishings are Holy, fit for kingdom work as *types* of spiritual processes going on within the future life of the believers who have the Holy Spirit indwelling them. For example, the Ark of the Covenant, a *type*, is actually a spiritual antitype of the human head, including the face. Please reread and digest that last sentence!

There, on the top of this Ark or box, one will find a lid that most references from the Bible call the mercy seat. It is also an antitype of the spiritual equivalent of the top of your head. The two *types* of cherubim are antitypes of our hands, the bridge of power between two worlds dispensing ministry by God's Holy Spirit!

Why would God create such veiled mystery in this tabernacle structure, and why would He conceal its true identity for all those years? The answer may be that a Holy God loves you and sent the "*Holy* One," Jesus, to show you your holiness at the time when we would need the sight to see! The holiness of Christ Jesus within you is a wellspring of living water and a barrier to sin that will more clearly point a way back to communion with the Father.

But first, God needed to establish some ways and rules for loving Him and knowing His Son. Abraham learned very early that God is a jealous God, requiring devotion and, failing this, a blood sacrifice for sin. At a later time, God called out His people from Egypt to worship Him and to deliver to them the law. Life for His chosen people would require living under His statutes, commandments, and remembrance of the Jewish testimony–their history. Once the nation Israel began to follow after God, we see that they fell away, complaining and entering into sin.

It is at this point that our tabernacle begins to take on the design and function of an instrument for the appeasement of a Holy God and His wrath for the sins of an unholy nation. Israel's relationship is secured by the offering of a blood sacrifice once a year in a place called the Holy of Holies. Sin was placed upon an animal called the scapegoat, which, when released into the wilderness, carried away the offences of the people. There is peace with God by His acceptance of this sacrifice, and forgiveness is reestablished for the worship of a Holy God. Long ago, these processes were *types*, while today we use these principles in our prayer without understanding their true significance as *antitypes*.

Though spiritual incidents requiring faith were hidden from human eyes in years past and may be referred to as *types*, God's intent was being satisfied by the process of building up the believer's faith. Today, by contrast, we are learning to behold the *antitypes* and their true purposes (the spiritual things they portrayed through all those years). What do you think it will do to our faith if we are allowed to gaze upon most of the deep spiritual truth? In these end times, will we learn Holiness in this way and be as strong for kingdom work as were many of those gone ahead of us?

It would seem that God saved some of the best of His purposes for these last days. Is this the day when the eye that did not see or the ear that did not hear is to be opened? If the message is straightforward, will we understand such plain communication? It doesn't require much faith to observe a thing as it stares right back at you. With our scientific understanding of the age we live in and our sophisticated education, we may require little of the faith once needed to understand the *antitypes* left in our world.

Let us consider that our faith in God through Christ is something we build upon through the years, something He desires. Also, if we are to assume we do not need much faith for the things of God's kingdom laid bare before our eyes, it would follow that we may not have much time to worry about building up our faith anyway.

I would like to briefly outline some of the spiritual concepts we have referred to above as *types* to bring clarity to holiness, prayer, and the tabernacle:

TYPE	ANTITYPE
Tabernacle	*Human Body*
Ark of the Covenant	Human Head
Mercy Seat	Top of Head
Before the Mercy Seat	Human Face
Cherubim	Human Hands
Golden Censer	Prayer from the Heart
Brazen Altar	New Heart (*koilia*)
Smeared Unguent	*christós*, Jesus' Blood

First John 2:20 (KJV) teaches, "ye have an unction from the *Holy* One, and ye know all things." Unction in the King James Version, and the New King James Version is translated "anointing." Is the title Christ used as a *type* of unction or blood? Blood is not only the cornerstone of Jewish history and Christianity but also the central theme of communion with a Holy God. Jesus' blood is not useful in a place called heaven (1 Corinthians 15:50), the place where His resurrected body lives. His poured out blood is alive, never to see corruption (Acts 2:31, Psalms 16:10), useful in this realm, most likely within the heart of believers, as well as a covering.

Christ Jesus is not only sealed within the hearts of born-again Christians but Christ is also spiritually sprinkled upon their heads and faces. A Holy God, most likely sees us through the mystery of His Son's blood within and upon us, and thus we are found Holy. Fellowship in prayer is welcomed, and through Christ's atonement we are viewed as spiritually Holy. We are justified from God's side and EMPOWERED by our application of this truth to stand before a Holy God!

Since you have heard, and your eye has seen, you may be better prepared to continue your reading and ask of Christ, "Where are you staying?" "He said to them, 'Come and see'" (John 1:38–39).

2

HOLY CHRIST

The wonder of the historic Jesus Christ, both God and human at His conception, is amazing beyond man's scientific understanding. The *Holy* One, Jesus Christ, came into the highly favored one, His mother Mary, by the Holy Spirit (Luke 1:35). Protestant Christian, Orthodox, Catholic, and Messianic Jew agree upon His coming by the power of God which overshadowed that blessed Mother. We see that Gabriel helped Mary understand this miracle in this way: "The Holy Spirit will come upon you, and the power of the Highest will overshadow you; therefore, also, that *Holy* One who is to be born will be called the Son of God."

We have seen that a Holy God requires sinless holy worshipers. Further, we shall see how a Holy God's wrath is appeased in the atoning work of Christ Jesus. In this work, the Holy Spirit seals Christ within a knowable place in the believer's body. By this power, Christ is then spiritually smeared upon a believer's face and head, gaining the creature "access" to God (Eph. 2:18, *prosagō(gé)* Grk.). It is as if His blood were a living fountain of holiness within us. Not only will we see that He lives within us by plan and power, due to His divine nature, but also our understanding of such indwelling through the intersection of the spiritual and the natural worlds will challenge our level of perception.

Our faith was put to work when we first learned that Jesus Christ was placed within Mary—spiritually. It doesn't take a scientific degree to understand the basics of an embryo's fertilization. Something beyond the current knowledge of science and identical to germination took place in Nazareth those many years ago. This faith of ours will be stretched further as we look to see if Christ Jesus was spiritually placed within us.

We understand that fertilization takes place on a very small stage within a woman's body, her womb. Because we know the truth of that historic event, it may not be unreasonable for us to observe some past, present, and future events as processes following the same pattern of this procedure.

Does Jesus' blood come into believers, and does the Bible tell us so? Should we look to reveal Bible text in ways that assume its message may be veiled, more suited for comprehension in a scientific age? If we are that generation, let's see whether these claims are justified and relevant to believers who want to be involved in deeper worship with their Holy God.

"These things we write to you that your joy may be full"
(1 John 1:4).

The *Holy* One, Jesus Christ, came to be one with us, and thousands witnessed His perfect life. Of all that has been written about Him, Old and New Testaments as well as the church age authors, it seems to me that the apostle whom Jesus loved, John, gives us a sort of super-spiritual glimpse into the living *Holy* Jesus Christ. So let us follow along, staying close behind John to see whether he will answer the question, "Where is Jesus staying?"

Though the following examination of the apostle John should not be viewed as comprehensive, some facts, however, compel us to reexamine his writings for clues in our quest to reform the errors found in some difficult interpretations of Scripture as we revisit the truth.

- John's comments rest upon the authority of his being an eyewitness of Jesus' ministry. John argues the accuracy of his doctrine in 1 John 1 based on the fact that he had "heard, ... seen [and] handled" Him.
- John may have lived the longest of the apostles, awaiting Jesus Christ's Second Advent or return. Therefore, his Gospel and his letters were spiritually off the chart. This fits well into our age of spiritual interest as these marvels overtake our lives.
- Lastly, if we believe* he was the author of the book of Revelation, it would mean that Jesus Christ and another divine entity like Gabriel visited John in the spirit and opened his eyes. These clarifying events not only opened his sight into the Holy realm, but they created complexities in his writings that scholars and commentators are still working to unravel.

This is the ground we will stand upon to look over to the

---

* Early Christian writers believed John wrote *Revelation*: Irenaeus, Clement of Alexandria, and Tertullian.

spiritual side as we examine John's use and structuring of the Greek text; as he points us toward the living, the indwelling, and the covering unguent of a *Holy* Christ Jesus.

> He Himself is the propitiation for our sins, and not for ours only but also for the whole world (1 John 2:2).

During the time of the writing of this verse, John was confronted, we believe, with various forms of false teaching. We read in verse 18, "even now many antichrists have come"; though interesting, we are not focused upon historical philosophies. We are searching for Jesus the Messiah, *Jehoshua* (Hebrew), which means: "Jehovah saves."

In the first part of verse 2, John gives us a very good clue to the nature of Christ Jesus, hinting at His whereabouts. The interpretation of propitiation says one thing to its readers in their day and to us, by application, something profoundly different.

Above all, propitiation speaks of the indwelling unguent of the *Holy* Christ Jesus! As this verse* assumes the indwelling sealed condition, it follows that John is speaking to God's Christian subjects. They are qualified to actively take, and, partially in the passive sense, to receive His saving gift. Once this unguent is sealed within the Christian, within his heart, such a substance has the benefits found in the Old Testament *types* as follows:

> He shall take some of the blood of the bull and sprinkle it with his finger on the mercy seat on the East side; and before the mercy seat (Leviticus 16:14).

---

* I hope that most readers will be aroused enough by the following assertions to do an in-depth study of 1 John 2:2, 20, and 27 on their own.

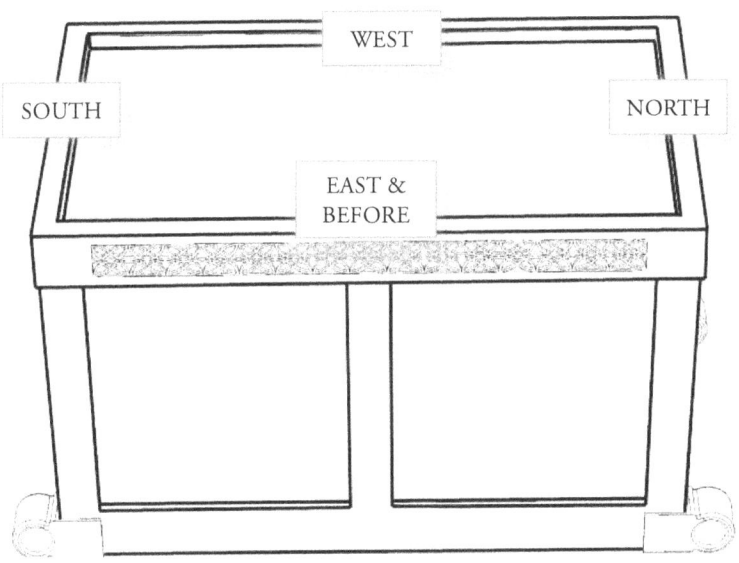

The spiritual application of this text assumes the blood of Jesus Christ, from out of the believer's heart, is spiritually smeared upon the top of the head and face of the one focused up and upon God. The deified state of Jesus' blood remaining in a place in time, defying natural laws, has precedent in the Biblical record. Our acceptance of Jesus (the man) walking on water, for example, and the application of His authority over time and place, helps us understand the possibility of sealed blood within the heart. Jesus set Himself apart, in the power of God, from the effects of gravity, the wind and waves most likely in a similar manner His blood refrains from co-mingling with ours. Can you see how the Bible helps us understand the indwelling possibilities of an interior Christ Jesus?

Two things happen as a result of this spiritual phenomenon:

(1) God's wrath is appeased* by vicarious atonement—Jesus' blood sacrifice. (2) The *Holy* Christ Jesus is the propitiation for our sins. In other words, He is the originator of the smearing as well as the unguent that is spiritually smeared on our face and head.

By definition, this is the deepest kind of mystery requiring a blending of contemporary understanding of Biblical truth and God's historical teaching incidents of the first covenant, or the Old Testament. How are we to understand God's plan without the aid of spiritual *types* like the symbolism of the Ark of the covenant? Let us focus in and narrow our search by moving along to this next verse.

> You have an anointing from the *Holy* One, and you know all things (1 John 2:20).

The first part of this verse helps us continue our focus on the indwelling Christ Jesus. We will not consider the last part of the verse, which reads either "you know all" or "you all know," according to various Greek scholars. Our concern, the anointing, is here redefined as an unguent, a smeared-on spiritual substance partially discussed as propitiation in verse 2. We should remember that His work, His sacrifice was an *antitype* for the blood of animals, a *type* of His sacrifice. If we mean to say that the *Holy* Christ Jesus lives within us as the Bible teaches,

---

* "Not that of appeasing one who is angry with a personal feeling against the offender; but of altering the character of that which, from without, occasions a necessary alienation, and interposes an inevitable obstacle to fellowship." Wuest, K. S. (1997, c1984). *Wuest's word studies from the Greek New Testament*, Grand Rapids: Eerdmans, 1 John 2:2.

we should consider the nature of such a deified life. (Later, we will consider at length more biblical detail upon these claims.)

Most Christians may believe that they are familiar with the indwelling Christ Jesus, yet they should not be confused with the resurrected God-Man, Jesus Christ seated in heaven. These deified forms of life may not be the same, not as we understand natural forms of life. The *Holy* Christ Jesus who indwells you in this realm does so by the mystery of shed blood and your acceptance of this blood as payment by His pain and death for our sin. 1 John 5:6, "This is He who came by water and blood"... reminding us of His appearing on the earth through His miraculous conception, perfect life, and subsequent death. These mysteries serve His Christian followers well, as our hope was confirmed on the occasion of His resurrection and new heavenly body. This Jesus Christ went on to His ascension with a body that is quite different from that in which born-again believers reside.

The ultimate truth that should be included in the application of 1 John 2:20 is that the *Holy* Christ Jesus, in the Spirit's power, is smearing us with the blood of the events of Christ's scourging and crucifixion. The power behind the implication of this blood is that it saved us once and continues to cleanse us in this dispensation, going before our confession of sin. Most of us affirm the terminology just mentioned, that God's wrath has been turned aside as we accept His vicarious atonement. Yet do we believe that such blood was spiritually available to us as we discussed in connection with Luke 1:28–35?

"You have an anointing from the *Holy* One" may be the coded terminology John is using to tell us where Christ Jesus is staying. Again, we are searching for the *Holy* Christ Jesus and where He resides. If we read the original language carefully, there is much to discover. For example, Holy is not accompanied by the word "One" in the original Greek. The addition of the word "One" by Bible scholars was an attempt to help us interpret the text. The insertion of the word "One" has been capitalized and is joined to the word Holy to support one popular and erroneous view that the verse is speaking about the Holy Spirit. I would offer two brief comments upon this controversial subject for brevity's sake before moving on with our search.

(1) John does not mention the Holy Spirit until verse twenty-four of the third chapter of this book. He is focused upon his beloved subject, the *Holy* Jesus Christ, who has dominated plainly the landscape of this second chapter along with God His Father. John records these words: "My little children, these things I write to you, so that you may not sin. And if anyone sins, we have an Advocate with the Father, Jesus Christ the righteous" (1 John 2:1). John tells us that "Jesus Christ is the righteous," may I say *Holy* one. He has not set upon a course to the Holy Spirit as His destination.

(2) By close examination, I have found Henry Alford and possibly Matthew Henry, of a long list of scholars, to be the only ones who support *Holy* as referring to Christ and not to the Holy Spirit. There may be others, but not among the ten or so commentators to whom I often resort.

"You have an anointing from the *Holy*." There it is, *put right* so that we may now look into this masterful Bible text of things spiritual. John writes in the *transitive*, "You have an anointing from the *Holy*." This term is telling us that *what you* "have" is transitional, on the move. Christ's blood, like living water from a well, affirms the transitive view. Well water comes up and is dispensed for the sake of something else. If Christ's blood is within us, it is transitional, and having come into believers spiritually, it will not dilute itself when dispensed.

Let's re-consider the *type* found in John 4, the woman at the well. Here is a fountain, pointing us to the simple truth that blood, an *antitype* of water in this illustration, is brought up for its gift of life as well as its gift of cleansing, both sin and conscience. This blood is the interpretation of an Old Testament *type* that dispenses itself not only to cover our sin but also encourages, and justifies our communion with God (Leviticus 16:14). Chapter 2 of First John is like a Greek stage set for a *transitive* scene to unfold; but we need to identify these players for who they are, because who they are expresses what they do.

Let us look more closely at what we *have*, or the identity of one of the players—*anointing*! If we interpret *anointing* as Old Testament royal *anointing*—Office-Bearer, Priest, and High Priest *anointing*—our list should also include *Holy objects*, smeared with oil and herbs. However, when we translate the New Testament *anointing* (to be rubbed on, smeared, a salve; an assignment and particular tasks), our interpretation of *anointing* is a confusing one. Do you see the tension among these various meanings to be somewhat troubling when trying to discuss *anointing*?

"*Christos* (χριστός), the Greek translation of the Hebrew and Aramaic word for Messiah, is also Anointed One. *Strong's* 5545 (χρισμα) [*chrisma* /khris·mah/] translates as "anointing" twice, and "unction" once."[1]

Did not our grandfathers use unction to suggest deified power in the hands of mankind? Again, we will remember that we are in consideration of the meaning of Holy with that of

Holy One. The definitions above should include an evaluation from a Holy object, or our *Holy* Christ Jesus over against Holy Spirit. The following observation from a leading Bible commentator is not totally correct:

"The word 'unction' is *chrisma*, (χρισμα) referring to that with which the anointing is performed, the unguent or ointment. Here it refers to the Holy Spirit with whom the believer is anointed."[2] This reference to the Holy Spirit, without the blood, and probably the Word, in fact, is incorrect although it is broadly accepted (See addendum 7).

We are not cleansed to stand before a *Holy* God, as the Bible records, with the unguent of the Holy Spirit. The application of the unguent of the *Holy* Christ Jesus may include actuating power by the Holy Spirit, but He, the Holy Spirit, is not blood. John is telling us that we are covered from *out of* the *Holy* to stand before a *Holy* God, having on our head and face the spiritual unguent of Christ Jesus. *Out of the Holy*, as we read the above, could imply a Holy object, smeared with oil and herbs as we saw in the Old Testament interpretation. In later chapters, there will be many textual references supporting the heart as this holy place.

To be certain, this is an extremely spiritual concept, yet because Christ's flesh (Blood) did not see corruption (Acts 2:31; Psalm 16:10), this anointing from the Holy is most likely a reference to His blood, and to His throne room, the *antitype* within believers. This, then, is a *type* of the most Holy thing within the tabernacle compound (brazen altar) of the Exodus account. John is not here talking about the Holy Spirit. These events speak of spiritual *types* that point us to the correct application. God's work is amazing in the design of His creatures, as our scientific boundaries are peeled back to reveal and confirm His glorious plan.

While we've learned a great deal thus far, many questions still persist as we review John's writings. In order to narrow our search for Christ Jesus and His dwelling place within, one of John's most powerful verses remains to be considered:

> The anointing which you have received from Him abides in you, and you do not need that anyone teach you; but as the same anointing teaches you concerning all things, and is true, and is not a lie, and just as it has taught you, you will abide in Him (1 John 2:27).

We will observe only the first parts of this pivotal verse. In the "anointing which you have received," John again states his earlier claim of the interior life of the unguent of a *Holy* Christ Jesus. Could the application of the atoning blood from His scourging be the interpretation of Paul's meaning in Galatians 2:20, "it is no longer I who live, but Christ lives in me"? I believe Jesus Christ revealed many spiritual things to Paul, yet the evangelist to the Gentiles was determined to build the church by faith and not by sight.

The following Bible study tools may help our sight as we focus on the themes surrounding *anointing*, and they should be helpful in understanding a *Holy* God requiring *Holy* blood for sacrifice and the forgiveness of sin. 1 John 1:9 tells us, If we confess our sins, He is faithful and just to forgive us and cleanse us. The practice of covering sin is done over and over again, while the opposite is true—Holy Spirit anointing, or oil commissioning, is done but once. Again, blood anointing is applied daily as a barrier to sin (1 John 1:9). Anointing: Vincent says, "An Unction (χρισμα)." Also, " . . . The root of this word and of χριστός, Christos is the same." And, "The anointing is from the anointed."

[NOTE: If detailed reading, including minor Greek phrasing, is a tedious experience, move ahead to the stop of page 42, starting with "In summation . . . " You may want to come back to this section another time.]

Let us move forward and look at the terms in verse 27. "The anointing which you have received from Him abides in you . . ."

(1) "have received:" (Gk. *lambánō, déchomai*) to take hold of something or someone, with or without force—"to take hold of, to grasp, to grab."[3] In the New Testament, to actively take, and, partially in the passive sense, to receive.[4]

Have received is past tense, speaking here of something we have already. We have *taken it*, the Greek is saying, *taken in hand, grasped*. These terms do well to identify the process of our past salvation and the sealed blood of Christ Jesus saving us eternally. It is as if we took hold—by faith—of this area of our lives by asking Christ Jesus to come in, thus qualifying us for what is to come. We know that the Holy Spirit was active in the process of our spiritual transformation. We also know that it was our choice and initiative for the implanting and sealing of a *Holy* Christ Jesus to take place. Concerning *have received*, the *Word Study Dictionary* says: "and, in the passive sense, to receive."

The Holy Spirit does have His powerful hand on these events even while we exercise our will—partially in the passive, yet firmly taking salvation—to *take hold* of salvation by faith when we first believe. Now John again reminds us of the *anointing we have*, and as we have said, it is in one form, the blood of salvation, but also it is in another form, that of the smearing.

(2) "*From*" is the next term in this verse which helps us to understand what He did, that we might know who He is and where He is staying. "... Anointing which you have received from . . .": In the Greek this word is the "preposition" apo, Str. 575 LN 89.122 ἀπό. It basically means the going forth or proceeding of one object from another.

Could we say it is blood from a place within us, a *type* of blood fountain? Is this blood sealed within us at the day of our transformation, sealed in the heart of every born-again Christian? The Greek-English Lexicon suggests "dissociation, implying a rupture from a former association—'*from, separated from.*'"[5] I think John has brought us round to his viewpoint as we consider first, our "*taking*" saving blood for salvation, *lambano*; second, blood spiritually proceeding "from" saving blood (How—we do not know), though our Bibles tell us it is like living water, one object from another; and now "Him . . ."

(3) "Him," is the third element in John's statement from out of verse 27:

"The anointing which you have received from Him" (Gk. αυτός autós): *the very one, the same. He . . . thyself, himself.* This earlier mentioned Lexicon supports "pertaining to that which is identical to something—'same.'" Jesus' deified blood from within you is the same as His anointing, same as His smeared blood upon you. Accordingly, this same blood from within one part of the body (The heart) is identical to the smeared blood upon another part of the body, the head. This is the amazing truth John is getting at, full of comfort and hope while clarifying the mystery of revealed truth.

In summation, Dr. Wuest reminds us: "We have an Advocate with the Father. "With" is pros (προς), "facing" the Father. Our Advocate is always in fellowship with the Father in order that, if the saint loses fellowship with Him through cherished and un-confessed sin, He might plead our cause on the basis of His precious blood and bring us back into fellowship again."

Reformation of doctrine is not so much an intellectual exercise as it is familiarity with Bible truth and proximity with God. Who of us truly understands the benefits of private praying, and getting alone and listening to "Our Father." God wants to communicate Spiritual truth with us, but we must maintain close and constant proximity with Him in Christ Jesus. Consider and compare the *types* found in the following verses with what we have just learned from the Spirit of Truth:

> Hebrews 10:19–20: "Therefore, brethren, having boldness to enter the Holiest by the *blood of Jesus*, by a new and *living way* which He consecrated for us, through the veil, that is, *His flesh*..."

> Leviticus 17:14: "...the life of all flesh is its blood."

> Colossians 1:27: "To them God willed to make known what are the riches of the glory of this mystery among the Gentiles: which is *Christ in you*, the hope of glory."

> Revelation 3:20: "Behold, I stand at the door and knock.

If anyone hears My voice and *opens* the door, I will *come in* to him and dine with him, and he with Me."

Ephesians 3:17–18: "... that Christ may *dwell in your hearts* through faith; that you, being *rooted* and *grounded* in love, may be able to comprehend with all the saints..."

1 Corinthians 12:13: "By one Spirit we were all baptized into *one body* . . ."

With a few strokes of the quill, John has formed cryptograms that have sent the intellectual Bible community into endless discussion over these passages. The above verses, 1 John 2:1–27, are filled with apparent contradictions and mystery. The text has been written and is revealed to our eyes; whether it is interpreted correctly, producing the proper application, remains to be seen.

Often, what we need is not more speculation, more chasing after old theories the answers of which leave us hungry for truth. John has written in a manner that demands dependence upon the Holy Spirit for relevant observation. Once we are able to see the text with the benefit of the entire life of Christ as our context, we are able to identify the truthful parts. We bring them from here, truth from there, and this patch-work of mystery is spiritually bound together out of the mind of Christ. Revealed mystery is linear, yet what is significant about this line, is its dependence on God's proper timing. The indwelling Christ is always on time.

The reality of the human structures of DNA relative to a *Holy* Jesus Christ, whose incorruptible blood was left behind for Christians, has amazing possibilities as we consider the mystery of Scripture. We have seen that the life of the flesh is in the blood and that His flesh did not see corruption. Scientifically, we know that one's blood contains the physiology, a sort of pattern of that person within its structures.

> To them God willed to make known what are the riches of the glory of this mystery among the Gentiles: which is *Christ in you*, the hope of glory (Colossians 1:27).

Where Jesus Christ is staying seems to be bound up in the question of His interior life and its whereabouts. It looks like the evidence is mounting up in the direction of an indwelling Christ Jesus quite different from what we have thus far understood through good Bible teaching out of the past.

As we conclude 1 John 2:27, we shall observe some physical and spiritual aspects of our final term: *abide*. "The anointing which you have received from Him *abides* in you." This Greek term, *meno*, is to be found in more abundance in John's writings than anywhere else in the Bible. While John will not tell us plainly where Christ Jesus is staying, in the following chapter he will point the tip of the entire biblical spear at the heart.

3

MENO

Loving a Holy God, I am pleased to remind you, is a commandment, and can only be done by the Holy Spirit through an indwelling *Holy* Christ. Why this is so has many wonderful answers for you to discover on your own, and you should spend as much time doing so as you find pleasing. Yet, in exhortation, I am pleased to point out for you the one primary reason why there is such a commandment: we are so strongly encouraged to love God in this way because it is simply *empowering*.

At times when I am exercising in the morning and my workout has become more trying than usual, I have learned to focus on Christ within for a kick start toward oneness, and the experience has become *empowering*. For another example, when my mind is troubled by the daily complexities within my streaming thought life, through past experiences and successes with the interior benefits of Christ within, I will focus on the singularity of the Christian's relationship in God and become *empowered* in my thinking processes.

There is *empowering* on both the physical and mental sides of the thing when we focus toward the interior, by Holy Spiritual processes, which move us upward from within the Christian heart. We should all be grateful to learn that God has also provided for our deeper psychological healing of the *conscience* through the *empowering*, cleansing blood of Christ.

Most of us have heard that we have been washed in blood. Is this the plain language that our parents used to describe what God had anticipated—psychotherapy? Have these instructions been coded in the Bible for all these years? We learn that the command to love God is a wholesome experience, that it is available to Christians by an active, interior Christ, for empowering healthy lives.

Most of us try to understand the things of God's kingdom, and their occurrences intellectually, while we depend less and less upon the Holy Spirit showing us truth. We evaluate most circumstances scientifically as our understanding and knowledge of life increase. We may even adopt principles and procedures, and find them useful, since they harmonize with the dynamics already at work in the complexities of the natural order of God's creation. We become proud of our accomplishments, even confessing our own wondrous part in their discovery. We apply our reason to these truths and attempt to make sense of them as we bring them into another structure of a building we've erected from the ground upward. I'm afraid any approach to reasoning out God's plan from the bottom up over against from the top down may prove mostly useless.

When I am empowered by the inward dynamics of Christ, it is not that I have discovered a truth or detected a secret to apply to my world. It is that I have learned that I can become empowered by a relationship from out of another world. By the power of that person, Christ and the Spirit of God, I can then be more vital in relationship with another like myself. Also, I am empowered to love God more deeply through abiding oneness.

The Shema (see Deuteronomy 6:4–5) helps us see this truth begun for those under the Old Covenant. We may look back and discover the roots of a system God taught His people concerning loving Him with their all. As God continues His lessons, we learn from His Son that the Shema also includes loving our neighbor as ourselves (Matthew 22:37–40; compare also with Leviticus 19:18).

Empowering seems to be a wonderful, supernatural phenomenon that has its purposes out of us and toward God and then toward others. The blood of Christ *empowers* us from *out of ourselves* supernaturally and *into others*, and the matter must be understood in continuity from the top downward and not so much from our perspective of placing these truths within the structures of the building we've erected from the ground upward. The seated, and resurrected Jesus remains connected to, and active with His body while He is in heaven, how I do not know. Yet His kingdom has come within us and we move in the light of His power. God does not need to wait for us to understand the dynamics of His church as we minister in power. Downward power is always available for ministry, whether we understand its spiritual process or not. By faith we have acted on saving blood, and God accomplishes the thing from then on. Understanding the building we erect, as outlined in this book, will only sustain, and add more power to this working structure as we become closer to God and learn to listen at His feet.

God created you and me to work well because of the blood

of Jesus applied to our hearts, to our inner parts, and not so well when blood is absent. God planned us to want a relationship with His Son. When He contemplated His creation, our human form in His image, He knew we would be imperfect creatures without His Son's empowering sacrifice. We have all heard that God has placed a vacuum in each human, a sort of inward desire that only His Son can fulfill. It should be clear to our understanding that our hearts contain this vacuum, and the Creator has always known that its filling would require the shedding of His Son's *Holy* blood—that has always been His plan.

Empowering dynamics and the blood of Christ must be understood as elements created especially for their usefulness in our lives that have become spiritually awakened. By God's Spirit, Christians can understand where Christ Jesus is staying and where He abides and, by trusting in this understanding, can become more *empowered*. Why, where, when, and how these dynamics apply to the spiritual life is closely tied to loving God. Loving God first—*a first things principle*—empowers the *second thing*, loving your neighbor as yourself.

How is it that we are really made to love God and our neighbor in the spiritual sense? This may require listening to God in a whole different way. All of God's family—those not in rebellion to His Son—are anxious for us to learn to apply these truths in a new way, the biblical way in which you love God. Should we expect all Christians to want to learn how to love the Father in a deeper way through His Son Christ Jesus? Most of us would be joyous to make a commitment to look deeper into the text, wanting the opportunity to experience God in a whole different way!

Again, one of the first questions we need to ask, out of the

Bible, for our progress, and empowering is this: "Where is Jesus Christ?" Is He really in heaven? It's a great question to ask and not too simple, for there are never many simple questions, nor are there any bad questions! Asking for clarification of the dwelling place of the God-Man Jesus can charge us with hope for today and the anticipation of our future Glory.

Historically the Bible tells us where Jesus walked, and millions flock to these sites in Israel to visit the places where His shadow once fell. This is not a bad thing to do, actually, for those who have traveled to the holy lands highly recommend the adventure. They will tell you of a noble, uplifting, and thrilling quest to close the reality gap with their beloved Savior, searching out His last footprints and gazing up in wonder from the general location where He ascended, while listening for the "two angels" inquiring of our curiosity and focus into heaven. John records these words for us as a reminder of His *ascension*: "I have not yet ascended to My Father" (John 20:17). All those anxious followers watching, and Acts tells us He was taken up! "While they watched, He was taken up, and a cloud received Him out of their sight" (Acts 1:9). He had gone into the clouds or presumably into heaven. This was witnessed by hundreds of spiritual souls.

Stephen, while being glorified during his martyrdom, looked up and saw Christ:

> He, being full of the Holy Spirit, gazed into heaven and saw the glory of God, and Jesus standing at the right hand of God, and said, "Look! I see the heavens opened and the Son of Man standing at the right hand of God!" (Acts 7:55–56)

He *looked up*! Here is this nagging question that must be asked if we are to have good observation added to our interpretation: If Jesus is in heaven as the text tells us, why does the Bible also refer to an interior Christ Jesus? Why does it tell us that Christ is within us?

> It is no longer I who live, but *Christ lives in* me (Galatians 2:20).

> "... the love of God has been poured out in our hearts by the Holy Spirit . . ." (Romans 5:5b).

> ". . . test yourselves. Do you not know yourselves, that *Jesus Christ is in you*? (2 Corinthians 13:5 NKJV)

> Behold, I stand at the door and knock. If anyone hears My voice and opens the door, *I will come in* to him (Revelation 3:20a).

Is the text really leading us to the conclusion that Jesus Christ stays within our hearts? It is easy to see why some would ask, "What in the world is going on here?" Are we to believe that Christ can be in two places at the same time—or for that matter in hundreds or millions of places at the same time? We are forced into a strange place of observation and interpretation of our Bible. Are there errors in the Word, a contradiction of terms, a form of heretical ideology, or have our scholars and textual experts misinterpreted, miscopied, or added to the text?

If Christ is in heaven and within our hearts at the same time, for this is what the Bible teaches, we should not be shy or reluctant to ask, "Where is this heart?" As we mentioned earlier in 1 John 2:27, abiding—*meno*—has put us on the trail of loving God and loving our neighbor. Yet we have come to a fork in the road and are struggling to find our way, to add one thing to another for our understanding and empowerment. Surely we are in need of help to become stronger that we might love God and love our neighbor. We are focused in on the heart, having asked the question, "Where is Jesus staying?"

> ". . . I will give you a new heart and put a new spirit within you (Ezekiel 36:26).

> "…God has sent forth the Spirit of His Son into your… hearts (Galatians 4:6).

> ". . . Out of [your] heart will flow rivers of living water (John 7:38).

> If anyone loves Me, he will keep My word; and My Father will love him, and We will come to him and make Our home with him (John 14:23).

This heart has become a very interesting place in light of the foregoing verses, for where the anatomy is concerned, these heart issues require more clarification. If we are to make any progress here, we must move forward and in a sense upward toward the supernatural. In the Greek, *koilia*, "bowels" or "heart" and even "womb," express to us a lower room within the body! Can you see why these questions need to be revisited for illumination of these highly charged claims? Our predecessors have given few comprehensive answers to this mystery.

If Christ is in heaven—for the Bible tells us so!—and if Christ is also in our hearts, for the Bible also makes this clear, it remains for us to solve the puzzle. The content of this truth is like the green orange: her peel was there for a purpose. Since the fruit has ripened in our season, turning the peel to orange, we shall take of her sweetness.

As we mentioned, there are no contradictions in the Bible, therefore Jesus Christ is in heaven and He is in my heart, in your heart, and in the hearts of Christians everywhere! Most of us understand this principle by the help of an advanced measure of faith and submit further investigation to the work of the Holy Spirit. This understanding includes some sort of spiritual *mechanism* that ties together our earthly sphere and God's heavenly kingdom—a sort of wormhole—powered by the Holy Spirit to place Christ within us, everywhere on earth, yet still within the heavens. Some such phenomenon would presumably make possible "*Christ in us*," for this is what we are told in Scripture:

> Do you not know yourselves, that Jesus *Christ is in you*? (2 Corinthians 13:5)

As we said earlier, most of us understand "Christ in us" and "in heaven" in some such way as just described. Others of us have not taken much time to consider how this could be; still others are contemplating these issues for the first time. Could it be said that most of the ones dismissing these questions are happy to declare: "Who cares? It really doesn't make a big difference in our faith. It's a mystery, and some mysteries are better left alone!" I venture to guess that a response like that is typical of many in the Christian community.

Is it a bad thing that we would not want to push out from an established pattern of belief and into areas that may best be left alone? Again, this routine opinion may reflect an unwillingness to risk bringing into our fellowship biblical error or false prophecy that on the surface does not appear to bear much fruit. Yet our faith has a unique opportunity to be just that, a faith that takes the Word at its face value. There is little doubt that we may need to simmer in these truths, allowing the Holy Spirit to guide us in these revelations while they bubble up from the heart and into the head.

Historically a considerable amount of text is reported to have been "revealed mystery"; in the strictest sense, however, it is revealed from God to man because it is included in the Bible, and it lies open before our eyes. It may not yet be interpreted or interpreted correctly, but it is revealed. Also the application of its truth may vary and be in question as well. Consider that because we see in a mirror dimly, is it still possible that the majority of experts believe they understand and can speak accurately regarding the most mysterious passages?

Concerning truth based upon the *majority opinion* and the *unsaved*, the Scripture tells us, "There is a way that seems right to a man, but its end is the way of death" (Proverbs 14:12 and 16:25).

Matthew Henry commented upon this text, "We must inquire what we ought to do, not what the majority do... [I]t is too great a compliment to be willing to go to hell for company!" With the church age moving steadily "end ward" (toward its climax) and with God's proper order becoming clear, the current stream of opinion often parts to reveal an altogether different light on the text than what the previous generations understood.

We must take care to confirm by Scripture itself while revisiting difficult truth. Scripture supports this method of reforming Truth, hence the two great reformations of the eighteenth and nineteenth centuries on the Continent and in America.

Meno, mena ("abide") are Greek terms reminding us that Christ is in us and we are in Him. This same Christ, while in us, is also seated at the right hand of the Father in a place called heaven. He is the God-man, and our understanding of abiding has little to do with whether it is true as we reason the thing out. It is true because the Bible says it is truth.

Jesus turned, and seeing them following, said to them, "What do you seek?" They said to Him, "Rabbi" (which is to say, when translated, Teacher), "where are You *staying*?" He said to them, "Come and see" (John 1:38–39).

The power to do the *first things*, loving God in Christ, is primary to walking in the faith. The blood of a *Holy* Christ has made access to God possible in ways the Apostles never thought possible. Rather than a dialogue on where He was staying, He taught them by simile, metaphor, allegory, and parables where His abiding place would be. His purpose all the while was to show them why He came and the place of His abiding. He could have said, *One day, I shall be staying in the heart of everyone who believes on Me.*

In our search to find the place where Christ is staying, the word *abide* (Greek: *meno*) should be a fundamental truth. I must say that it may not be such a fundamental truth after all; rather, it is revealed mystery of the troubling kind. John uses this term almost exclusively among the authors of the New Testament because of its super-*Spiritual* implications. Understanding our world as a physical *and* spiritual reality over against a physical reality alone makes good Bible sense, but it also leaves us dependent on the same Bible for spiritual interpretation. This as you may know, is a good thing; read your Bible! Our most powerful relationships are in the spiritual realm, and Christ commands us to go to such a place daily. *Meno* is that place where the power of God resides. The following quote is from the French Protestant pastor Adolphe Monod, who wrote, "Too much taken up with our work, we may forget our Master; it is possible to have the hand full, and the heart empty."

> At that day you will know that I am in My Father, and you in Me, and I in you (John 14:20).

> He who eats My flesh and drinks My blood abides in Me, and I in him (John 6:56).

The *Bible Knowledge Commentary*, with its roots in Dallas Theological Seminary, says of John 6:56: One who partakes of Christ enjoys a mutual abiding relationship with Christ. He **remains** (*menei*) **in** Christ, and Christ remains **in him**. —*Menō* is one of the most important theological terms in John's Gospel ...The Father "remains" in the Son (14:10), the Spirit "remains" on Jesus (1:32), and believers "remain" in Jesus and He in them ...A believer enjoys intimacy with and security in Jesus. Just as He has His life from **the Father,** so believers have life **because of** Jesus.[6]

Anywhere in the above commentary would have seemed to me to be a good place to explain an association of the ascended Jesus Christ in heaven with His ensuing earthly ministry, but commentators rarely handle spiritual questions of this nature.

What we do find useful from this commentary, among other things, is a clue pointing us to where the *Holy* Christ is staying. This clue reminds us that "the Spirit 'remains' on Jesus" (John 1:32). This is immensely helpful to us in our present search, and in the chapters that follow. We shall see later that the Holy Spirit remaining on Christ is a *type* found in the tabernacle.

The relationship of the Holy Spirit to Christ helps us identify the place where Christ is staying, for Scripture confirms by itself the place of this alliance. For now, we shall observe only this one thing: that the Spirit will rest upon the *Holy* Christ. Luke, in his Gospel (3:22), tells us that the Holy Spirit "descended in bodily form, like a dove, upon Him." The dove, *in bodily form*, supposes not only a spiritual transformation into a physical manifestation but the symbolism of the power of God willingly entering into a *permanent* relationship with Christ to offer us His peace.

Are we to understand that a *Holy* Christ should be found in proximity to the Holy Spirit once and for all in this same way—the Spirit "upon Him"? Should we wonder whether this is to be a one-time event or whether it represents a spiritual relationship that will continue while Christ is in the flesh (Matthew 3:16; Mark 1:10)?

If it is true that we should look for Christ in a place that would allow the Holy Spirit to be upon Him, we can, by Scripture, confirm that that place may be the human body. For Scripture confirms that both the Holy Spirit and the *Holy* Christ are indwelling. In later chapters we will confirm these truths, but for now, we have learned that the Holy Spirit should be in a *typical* relationship with the *Holy* Christ. We shall see that the Holy Spirit is to be upon the *Holy* Christ, and this is most significant. Before we look at some biblical dictionary definitions of meno, let us sum up what we have come to know of that place where the *Holy* Christ is staying. We have found that Jesus Christ who ascended into heaven is the Christ within believers. We have seen also that Christ Jesus mysteriously abides within us, and some may understand this to take place through His saving blood. We have found that the Bible speaks of the atonement of blood as a covering of sin. We know by Scripture that Christ dwells within the heart, and by inference, we believe this to mean that He has a ministry within believers, inside the brazen altar, an *antitype* of the heart. Lastly we believe that the Holy Spirit came upon the Christ, and it can be assumed that this is the power of His ministry, which in turn is an *antitype* of the laver, the Spiritual power of our lives.

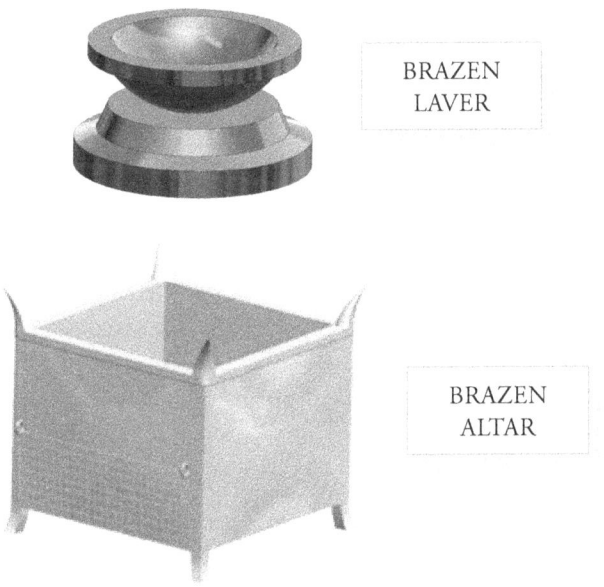

BRAZEN LAVER

BRAZEN ALTAR

Our Bible dictionaries tell us many revealing things about the word *meno*: "to remain, abide, dwell, live. (I) Intrans., to remain, dwell. (1a) Of place, i.e., of a person remaining or dwelling in a place (3306. μένω *ménō*)."[7]

"This word means a. 'to stay in a place,' figuratively 'to remain in a sphere,' b. 'to stand.'"[8]

"To remain in the same place over a period of time—'to remain, to stay.'"[9]

"The verb μενω [*menō*] (to abide) expresses continual mystical fellowship between Christ and the believer as in 15:4–7."[10] (Abide in Me ... I in you ... (the) branch ... (the) vine ...)

The enthroned Jesus Christ of Nazareth is recorded to be the same One to whom John makes reference in 1 John 2:2, 20, and 27. This is the *Holy* Christ. This is the *Holy* spoken of in 1 John 2:20, and we learn that He abides within us in a place that we can know. The enthroned Christ is the indwelling *Holy* Christ having come in power from on high, abiding in the hearts of those born from above. Paul discusses abiding in differing ways from that of John's writings, so let us compare their handling of abiding oneness in the following chapter.

4

ABIDING ONENESS

It may be helpful for us to remember that it is more than probable, based on the extreme spiritual nature of John's Epistles, that he wrote after he was invited to come up and see where the *enthroned* Jesus Christ was staying. Revelation 4:1 tells us:

> [B]ehold, a door standing open in heaven. And the first voice, which I heard, was like a trumpet speaking with me, saying, "*Come up here*, and I will show you things which must take place…"

As we consider the invitation to the *Apostle* John encapsulated in the above phrase: "*Come up here*", His experiences become extremely helpful to our understanding of abiding oneness and to the probability of these various forms of spiritual transportation. Our physical bodies can be fixed upon the earth (physical realm), while our new heart helps our upward spiritual progress in oneness towards God. The apostolic experience John had, we will remember, was recorded and sealed in the text. We should not expect experiences such as this in the church age, or we will need to rewrite the Bible. That will not happen!

The view from on high, not so much every detail and mystery of the place, gives John the understanding necessary to construct a document that conceals mystery to some (non-Christian community) while revealing to others the inner structure of a spiritual world available to Christians. This structure is a spiritual column called "abiding oneness." Its heavenly Spiritual workings are not that well understood by Christians, but its earthly workings are coded throughout the Bible.

Paul, quoting Isaiah 64:4, tells us,

> We speak the wisdom of God in a mystery, the hidden wisdom which God ordained before the ages for our glory, which none of the rulers of this age knew; for had they known, they would not have crucified the Lord of glory. But as it is written: "Eye has not seen, nor ear heard, nor have entered into the heart of man the things which God has prepared for those who love Him" (1 Corinthians 2:7–9).

It would seem that at Christ's appearance, these things the eye and ear have not apprehended are now suddenly available in the Son.

Paul, also having been taken away to the spiritual realm, understands heavenly things in this deeper way (2 Corinthians 12:2, 6). Both John and Paul see the water at the bottom of the well in ways equally suited toward their ministry goals.

Paul sees the water in the well and by it evangelizes the Gentiles and builds the church on Truth. John sees the circumstances surrounding the "woman at the well" as *types* of spiritual phenomena, reminding us that abiding in Christ Jesus, may well be abiding in the blood. Both men view Christ's blood in the Spirit and the truth. Paul speaks with the building blocks of faith, while John's spiritual sight may see faith failing and may have in view a revival for the end of the age of the Gentiles. Such times are those in which we may need insight: the eye that we spoke of earlier that did not see and the ear that did not hear (1 Corinthians 2:9–10).

If we believe that Christ is enthroned in heaven as well as indwelling Christians, what other evidence is there for us to confirm these assertions? It's never too late for us to return to 1 John for more spiritual insight; after all, John was there!

> You know that He was manifested to take away our sins, and in Him there is no sin. Whoever abides in Him *does not sin*. Whoever sins has neither seen Him nor known Him (1 John 3:5–6).

The troubling nature of this verse speaks out of a controversial principle of the sinless. We already know that "All have sinned." John reminds us earlier,

> "If we say that we have no sin, we are deceiving ourselves, and the truth is not in us" (1 John 1: 8).

On the one hand, John tells us that we sin. On the other hand, he says that if we abide in Jesus, we do not sin. I am not a

Bible scholar, but I do know this: the question hangs on whether we abide in Jesus, whether we remain in such a deep relationship with Him that sin cannot affect our abiding relationship. Such a state will exist if the mind is set upon such wonderful tasks, and is so completely occupied with the business of oneness that nothing else but the glorious oneness of relationship with Jesus occurs.

The mind is so occupied, in a state of rapture and in ecstasy, that sin is barred at the door. Again, the mind must be occupied with its multifaceted task of looking into the name of God beyond all distraction. Do you see that we learn to become stronger, learn how our focus should be on "abiding," upon staying, upon remaining? It means our focus is steadily on a joyous union with Christ, and this fixed purpose sustains the fortification against sin.

John continues speaking to the spiritual man on multiple levels that sustain the appetite of new learners as well as the ones looking longer and deeper at these mysteries found in 1 John, chapters 2-3. Christ Jesus, blood sacrifice, and abiding are his centerpieces of controversy. John gives us an impossible puzzle to solve here in 1 John 3: 6. Impossible, that is, to fit the pieces into a mold if you resort to the tools of the natural world. You must skip over this verse and verse 9 if you are not willing to open up your Spiritual eyes and look into the Spiritual workings of the inner man or woman.

"Whoever abides" is a discussion upon a place within the human body called the heart. Instead of talking around this place, as did the other disciples, John forces us to realize that there is such a place and it is a *type* that he chooses to illustrate by means of the difficult topic of the sinless. We soon find ourselves caught up chasing our tails when we attempt to resolve the question of the sinless person. 1 John 1:8 has barred the door to the sinless person and forced us to search in the corridor of abiding.

Either we rewrite the text, or else we ignore it and move along in ignorance. Since this is not what those who seek after the truth are interested in, let us follow after John in his third chapter; Leave the sinless to those in the world system struggling in their rebellion of the truth, and let us focus on abiding.

A good question to ask at this point would be "If I am a born-again believer, do I not abide in Him because of my regeneration?" According to 1 John 3:6, 9, " Whoever abides in Him does not sin." Taken at face value, this scripture seems to be telling us that abiding speaks to a deeper realm of Spiritual dwelling. By our position in Christ, most believe we do abide. This I will not contest, yet I would add that such a oneness is a casual drifting in and out, sometimes deep, sometimes not. This sort of abiding generally happens by the Spirit falling upon us despite our efforts. Again, we do not exclude the special occasion of the Holy Spirit falling upon us at His arbitrary times, but remember, we are talking about "whoever abides," or the one who desires to initiate the process of oneness.

The following statement develops this abiding principle: "God has sent His only begotten Son into the world, that we might live through Him" (1 John 4:9). As we abide in Christ Jesus, our life is lived through another life: God's life, God's person, Christ Jesus. So the answer is yes, you must be saved or born from above. While the nature of the Christian is altered by the presence of God's own Son, Christ Jesus, within you, we are talking about sonship and its rights. Do you demand entrance into God's presence? Should you be so bold as to lift the shoulders, throw the head back, and move upon this purpose? Consider from where, each morning, you are to begin this campaign. While standing in the natural realm, your prayers are wrestling against "principalities, against powers, against the rulers of the darkness of this age, against spiritual hosts of wickedness in the heavenly places" (Ephesians 6:12). Also remember Paul's admonition in the 18th verse: "praying always with all prayer...in the Spirit."

Just as I am able to reach out and take my wife's hand in the natural, we must learn that John is telling us that we may also reach into the spiritual realm and take hold of oneness. Demand your rights of sonship against the opposition while the roar of encouragement echoes through the courts of heaven. Scripture is telling us that abiding oneness is happening from the top down, but it goes deeper into whether you exercise your sonship from the bottom up. This is not a casual drifting into a mental or emotional state, but this thrust of truth is all about advancing into the proximity of God. This is a function of spiritual knowledge and the practice of such knowledge for useful progress in the spiritual realm.

> You are not in the flesh but in the Spirit, if indeed the Spirit of God dwells in you (Romans 8:9).

While this verse sums up the born-again Christians, it goes on to say,

> Now if anyone does not have the Spirit of Christ, he is not His. And if Christ is in you, the body is dead

because of sin, but the Spirit is life because of righteousness (Romans 8:9–10).

Just because one can cite Scripture that suggests that one is "in the spirit," it does not follow that one really understands the nature of spiritual "in-ness." Remember that most of our lives are lived in the vanity of our minds, which babble onward from daybreak to sunset, hardly visiting the spiritual places of the heart. For example, in John 10:3, 9 we read, "The sheep hear [the shepherd's] voice ... [and they] will go in and out and find pasture." If you are born again, you are not "unborn" so that you may go "out" again from relationship with Christ. By the blood of Christ Jesus, the Holy Spirit has saved and cleansed you, and you are not required by Jesus Christ's words to go in and out of your cleansed condition.

Jesus suggests a deeper principle in this swinging gate parable. It has little to do with reason, the thinking process, logic, or meditation upon a mystery. The mind has its role, but it is not dominant so much as it is guardian, watchman, and strong tower for an activity of relationship with God.

Thus we have this eternal lifeblood that non-believers do not have. This kind of access, for fellowship with the Father, is not such as Adam had in the garden. Sin has broken man's fellowship with God. Today, *we* have a choice to be either spiritually in or out of pasture, and aware of that relationship with God in Christ. Our consciousness of moving into an abiding relationship from the bottom up is determined by our willingness to go there. God's relationship with us in Christ Jesus is ongoing from the top down.

You are able to enter into oneness because of this once-asked-for-and-received fact of Christ Jesus in you, and that position is there whether or not you think upon it or act upon its family ties. This is about abiding in Him consciously, and then consciously living for the purpose of intentionally doing His will.

These conscious acts are cultivated while alone with Him, which is the place where sin may have no room, sway, or moment. The practice of oneness applied to the daily life of the believer is the place where most find this truth troublesome, and then run into problems. The abundance of the confusion that is found in this business of abiding oneness is cleared up when its place of exercise is understood.

Abiding is first "a belief" in God's plan that recognizes discipline and progress toward depth in one's relationship with Him. These principles begin and take place in the heart, Christ's home. That is not to say that none but those disciplined in oneness abide! All those born from above experience relationship. Rather, it is the quantity of our daily use of authority (conscious use of our sonship rights) and exercise of these rights toward power, (released by the Holy Spirit as He acts behind our faith). It is the quantity of time with God that is the essential issue here. The quality of our relationship with God is only relevant from our perspective.

In consideration of quantity of relationship, some prayer warriors spend hours in supplication and by such effort are unwittingly transformed into abiding oneness by the persistence of prayer which pushes one into proximity to God. This is the exception to the rule of "knowingly" and "willingly" moving from the natural realm into the spiritual, which is the place where we have come to understand the abiding question.

Through the Spirit of Christ Jesus, we know that this natural life that we're born into has within it a spiritual aspect, a spiritual dimension. We who have the Holy Spirit, have Christ Jesus the living God within us as well. We can shift from the natural dimension into the spiritual dimension at will. These are powerful words for a powerful proposition. Not many of us openly speak of traveling within spiritual dimensions, yet various forms of the spiritual state of being are accepted without question. For example, by faith we fall asleep entering another dimension, assuming we shall awake in a few hours, and don't give it a second thought. Some of us daydream, caught away by the thought life and into another realm. What do we say about visions? The Bible tells us that in the latter days our young men will see visions; nothing new here. These things are all around us. We should open up our spiritual eyes and look.

Prophets of old, including Paul, had visions. While we admit that these spiritual things may be real, we are also reluctant to admit they are relevant to us. We are more likely to distance ourselves from them, as if they were intended for other circumstances and other times. We believe in their historical reality, but we are unwilling to believe that such phenomena have a role in our current scientific age.

The facts suggest a spiritual world, a spiritual pathway, and the Bible as our spiritual guide. As Philip was directed in Acts 8 to assist the Ethiopian eunuch, this seeker after the heart of God, so we too shall have our Philip, the prophetic community, to show us the Heart of the Father for our day. The question is what we ourselves are *willing* to do. The Christian, having the Holy Spirit, is endowed by faith to initiate this jump from natural to spiritual dimension, and without doubting become "sinless." In fact, God leaves this initiative to His creatures, specifically to teach them to freely choose to enter God's dimension, enter His throne room, and abide in oneness with Him. "Whoever abides in Him does not sin" (1 John 3:6).

If there is to be a new covenant, its place must be brought down from on high and into the natural, physical world. God has not sent His only begotten Son into the forest to find a tree to abide in, not sent Him into the sea for the fish, into the earth as seed in the dirt. Jesus is come into us, into our hearts to stay! Jesus indwells people within a place spoken of clearly and plainly in the Bible. Although we have read about such a place and have heard the preacher teach about such a place, most readers will remain unconvinced that such a place exists. I am hopeful that this group of followers of Christ will in due time come up to speed alongside the prophetic community.

Our next opportunity to observe what the scripture was saying to our former generation in contrast to what the text may be saying to our generation concerns the misuse of terms, phrases, and assumptions concerning the tabernacle and its furnishings. There is a tremendous amount of information out there that handles the tabernacle in a wide variety of ways. Many excellent scholars, men of letters, and others have given good treatment to this structure found in the Old Testament. There must have been a tremendous amount of study, research, and collaboration brought to bear upon the nature of its purpose and place. Sadly, most of the work misses the simplicity of the architect's design.

While it seemed we were moving right along, making good progress, I must confess I can almost hear some of you saying, "Now where is this wild goose chase taking us?" The route we are taking shall be at first a bit steep, narrow, and seemingly bottomless. Without many travelers of our day upon this road, it is to be expected that we shall be nearly alone here. In addition, such rough terrain is made rougher because of the perfectly sensible fear of losing credibility, and becoming heretical. While at first we may appear so, as we connect the dots, the mystery will unwind itself much like the ripening orange we mentioned earlier. We are face to face with prophetic truth, and it is the progress toward a powerful God in Christ Jesus that strengthens our ministering and shows us the love of God.

The following Bible interpretations, in the next chapter to be discussed, are in need of reforming. They should be brought out and into our day as if they were the same wine of the ancient patriarchs, old and fermented, hardly touched since left upon the table of the upper room. The amazing truth of these time capsules will minister to you for exhortation, edification, and comfort.

We have looked to Scripture to understand the possibilities of a relationship with God, through the saving blood of a *Holy* Christ abiding within our hearts. These first steps taken were slow and methodical because they move astride our belief systems. By Scripture, John helped us reveal sacred truth lying just below the surface. Let us turn to Moses the prophet and see what physical *types* he has left along the way for our examination.

5

GOLDEN LAMPSTAND

The interpretation of the Holy Place in the tabernacle is most closely associated with the application of His atonement by caring Christians in the lives of others. One born again Christian touches one lost soul for the cleansing of sin. This one caring Christian, having been made perfectly holy by blood sacrifice, serves another one of God's creatures. Service is done in the flesh world by way of spiritual processes God chose to illustrate in His tabernacle design.

The interpretation of this divine transaction carried out in the middle place of the ancient tabernacle, the Holy Place, was carried out in the physical world by the priest. Today, by application, it is our spirit that is the workman represented as an *antitype* of this priest. The historical Hebrew Levite and priest would minister for the supplicant, assisting in the sacrifice, and ensuring that the sacrifice pleased God. Today, it will be helpful if we view the three major furnishings—the table of showbread, the golden lampstand (menorah), and golden censer (incense bowl)—as the spiritual offices where creature-to-creature ministry takes place.

In the Holy Place, one finds the showbread on the left or the north. One's heart is also on one's left. The menorah, with oil lamps on the right (the south), kept trimmed and illuminating the tented chamber. A friend of mine, helping with an early draft, offered this observation: "This layout foreshadows the cross, with the lowest point at one's feet, the Holy of Holies at the head, and the bread and lamp on either side, slightly up from the middle, as well picturing the ultimate sacrifice of Jesus on the cross." This is just one of the many interpretation possibilities found in the Bible in discussion of furnishings, including the menorah which typifies a person standing, arms lifted in praise. So let us look at the rooms inside this tabernacle for more of our details, starting with the place of worship.

The menorah was a complicated structure of seven wick-fed oil lamps that were to be kept burning during the day. Beyond all dispute, the oil symbolizes the work of the Spirit of Truth, the Holy Spirit, illuminating God's Word, the Son of God—Jesus Christ. The oil feeds the light and keeps it lit, but only insofar as this natural illustration is concerned. Christ needs no supplies brought up from the rear to supply Himself or His efforts; He is God, self-sustaining, the light of the world. Aaron trimmed the lamps every morning, first thing in the morning. So should we also, every morning, let our light shine unto the Father in willing praise, sacrifice, and offering. The wick was a cloth twine that worked along with the oil to produce a valuable service, lighting the inner places. Our light should be a result of our work, but only if that work is infused with the oil of the Holy Spirit.

The light in the Holy Place was one stem with three pairs of branches, making seven candles total. One can see a parallel between these three pairs and the three pairs of gifts in Isaiah 11:2, "The spirit of the Lord shall rest upon him, the spirit of wisdom and understanding, the spirit of counsel and might, the spirit of knowledge and of the fear of the Lord." These three pairs, John tells us in Revelation, are in Christ's right hand. The Holy Spirit, which He has given us, rests upon Him. As we look closely at the menorah lampstand, it becomes very clear that such a device has no standing without its base. Jesus, a *type* within the base has become the illustration God is making of the lampstand and its spiritual purpose. The Holy Place is where the spiritual work of Christ conforms the pairs to God's will, creature to creature. Today, our hands reach into the lives of others helping to conform them by sanctification, thus becoming more like Jesus, the first Adam (1 Corinthians 15:45).

As we are considering the menorah standing in the middle room, the Holy Place with the one single center candle, we find the additional six candles forming the pairs. "The spirit of wisdom and understanding" are the outside pair, possibly gifts of administration and application of orderly human activities. "The spirit of counsel and might" are the next pair. *Counsel* can include prophetic advice or warning. All good advice is from God in purpose and plan. *Might* is for strength (*exousia* and *dunamis—divisions of the concept of power, Grk*) to implement and protect alive the voice of God to overcome adversarial opposition. This sort of fight always takes place upon the spiritual plane, though its ruckus is manifest in the world system. The last pair is "knowledge" and "fear of the Lord." *Knowledge* is to know the Word of God, the basis of supernatural insight, while *fear of the Lord* is man's appropriate response to relationships with God's creatures. If God loved my neighbors enough to send His Son to love them, how should I act?

Teachers and preachers understand that the Word of God saves lives. They are concerned that God's Word "will not" save the lost because they will not hear—for they will not listen. Hell is for those who will not listen, and this is the sort of motivation that causes our loving preachers to fight for the lost. This is the fear that drives the evangelists, teachers, and preachers into ministering to the weak and dying with their all. Fear of the Lord is always at work in the preachers and teachers who stand in the gap for the weak and biblically ignorant and naive. (2 Corinthians 5:11)

One of the things I most loved about J. Vernon McGee's lectures was his candid statements. It was not unusual to hear him say, "I'm alone on this ground!" referring to other Bible teachers, scholars, and textual experts on any number of Bible topics. When he would start down that road, you knew it would be a bit bumpy, steep, and filled with excitement. I am not Dr. McGee, though I believe that now and again I've spent time on that same road; I'm sure the bumps are just around the corner concerning the lampstand and its interpretation.

Consider all Israel wandering in the desert for forty years, the conquest of the Promised Land, the eventual building of the temples, the one built by David's son Solomon and King Herod's later edifice.

We see that the tabernacle/temple was the preferred means by which Israel came before her God. Also we will discover that the golden lampstand functioned for hundreds of years as a symbolic reference to the spiritual activity designed by God. Every time Aaron or another priest lit those lamps in the morning (it was done first thing), God was speaking out by way of a *type* toward the church age phenomenon of "private spiritual worship" and corporate worship.

The tone and tenor of sacrifice tempered by the element of the years and *number of times* God required this process of lighting and relighting of the menorah was an amazing statement, harking forward to His plan as it anticipated your presentation at court in Christ Jesus. This concept is expressed in Romans 5:2, ". . . through whom [Christ] also we have access." In the Greek "access" is *prosago* and might suggest the one who introduces you at court—a spiritual introduction of the Most High illustrated by the center lamplight (Ephesians 2:18; 3:12). Repetition of this nature reveals the deepest kind of teaching, and its unmistakable purpose should always be considered closest to the heart of God as our eyes are opened at last. Blood spiritually smeared upon the head and the face is what makes our access possible before a Holy God by the One—the *Holy* Christ Jesus introducing us at court.

At this level you will better believe with your heart, when it is shocked into the reality of a divine relationship with a God in love with His creatures. The primary flame of Isaiah 11:2, the "Spirit of the Lord" flame—the one in the middle of the golden lampstand—is screaming out of those past centuries and toward this abiding pathway to the Father as we are led out in the Son. Somehow you know of this grand linkage, and I'm not surprised, for our churches have done a great service in providing us with proper teaching on these ancient statutes and commandments and the testimony on the way to oneness with the Father.

The text will always support good teaching, yet has the Holy Spirit, in the eyes and ears of the Christian community, shut up their understanding, so to speak? Has this time, the times before the "Great Day of the Lord," been a time of revealing His clear speech out of the Son for such a great day? If you would know the Son, vowing to look deep for understanding of His Word, you are the ones the Father seeks. You are the ones who really love Him, seeking Him with all your heart. This primary lamp must be followed to its spiritual ends and not left on the scholar's bookshelf.

This primary lamp is not just a shadow and not just a *type* of a heavenly article. It is not even just the obvious instrument to light a room in an old tent. We are face to face with the power of God come by His divine purpose, that you and I may experience oneness with Him. If you could not read, as was the case with most of our early Orthodox or Catholic brothers and sisters, the way to the Father would still be there for you to see, touch, and wonder at its amazing statement in the Menorah Icon. (Remember that almost all the early believers in Christ were defined as either Orthodox or Catholic—members of communions that, still to this day, maintain a strong iconographic tradition, Without reading skills, the image was and still is powerful to convey the message.

In the following illustration you will find a menorah lampstand with a few of the ornate segments subdued. In Exodus 25 we are told what sort of dimensions Moses was to follow as he created from sight and supervised into physical being the object that is clearly the *type* which points our heart singularly upward to celebrate the Creator, God the Father.

SINGLE CANDLESTICK

What is to be understood about this conductor of spiritual power from within us is that, as mentioned earlier, the lamp will not function without a stand, its base. Like any design of a working device, for the thing to be relevant and purposeful, its end must have been clearly seen by its designer. Without an understanding of why the object exists, it will never achieve lasting, beneficial service. For a lamp to light its surroundings, you must put the flame on the top of the structure and have its height in mind so that its base may be broad enough to help support the flame. As Christians, we love to talk about Jesus, or we should love to anoint our conversations in His light, an application of the lampstand. In Scripture there are many illustrations, stories, and testimonies pointing to the fact that fountains have their source, light emanates from its source, and wheat by way of death becomes the bread of life. Jesus is that supply, as together we bring up that which is pleasing to the Father... Oneness, I in You and You in me—*meno*, abide.

Such is this illustration of the center menorah flame burning out by way of our faith the holy praises celebrating God's Holy name. Sealed, the figure of a permanent reservoir of light taken up in oil which fashioned first this world and continues to fashion and fit for righteousness our heart worship. The praise of mortals, like lamplight, may never be able to sustain the vigorous duty of burning themselves into abiding oneness throughout the day, yet our instruction encourages us to try.

> God is the Lord, and He has given us light; bind the sacrifice with cords to the horns of the altar (Psalm 118:27).

Arise, shine; for your light has come! And the glory of the Lord is risen upon you (Isaiah 60:1).

Once we are given sight of the furnishings in the temporary temple, our way is clear to follow and interpret their meaning for application. How should God make His point if not by blowing your mind with something like the tabernacle's furnishings, indicative of the spiritual offices at work within Christians? The lampstand is primary to private prayer, and it is now time for the simplicity of its true purpose to be brought into the prophetic circles for examination. (You may find an animated graphic at: www.TabernacleHome.com)

We are looking into the "first things," the light directly supported by the base of the center lamp, which speaks of Jesus and ourselves burning in oneness. The physical dynamics of today's candle, wax melting at the flame, falls short figuratively. We find that where there is understanding of the spiritual nature of the temple and the spiritual furnishings for spiritual work, the oil that is illustrated in such work is giving testimony to the power of the Holy Spirit. It is the Holy Spirit through Christ who assists you in taking the light to the world. The usefulness of the center lamp is the greatest wonder attached to the greatest story ever told, for the single lamp speaks prophetically of intimacy with the Father and the Son. It leads us back to the garden relationship God has so desired for us. He longs to know us in an intimate way, every morning, alight with burning news of the life we have in His Son, Christ Jesus, told in the simplicity of Bible verse, and psalm to His praise. Later we will discuss the concept of the single light and the relationship it signifies in more detail.

The base of this lamp and its height work to help it light the surroundings, and though it is not found in this "form" in the sanctuary, also called the *Holy Place*. Normally, there are joined to the above illustration three sets of couplet branches. Here they are removed to illustrate the "first things": love God with all your heart. Prophets are subject to prophets as our great apostle to the Gentiles has taught us in 1 Corinthians 14. The full lampstand, as a picture of purpose, has been lying around on our desktops, libraries, and charts of biblical illustrations for years, and it's obvious nature is a revelation to the Christian community (1 Corinthians 13:2).

Jesus Christ gave us the perfect prayer of praise, worship, and adoration when His disciples asked Him to teach them to pray. Jesus taught the prayer that the Father loves to hear in the fire of the Holy Spiritual language from within the heart, outward, by way of heaven's door. Sweet, sweet smell of the blood of Christ Jesus and the Spirit blended within you and me, the sacrificial doorway of flaming oneness. We offer up Holy spiritual praise to the Father, and of the Lamb, a ministry out of our souls. Are we not giving God our substance, and does He not tell us His reward is with Him (Isaiah 40:7–10; 62:11)?

Matthew 6:9–12 begins "Our Father," or, as the original Greek indicates, "Father of us." We learn that Christ spoke these words to His disciples and clarified His meaning by reminding them that they were to be alone in their closet while praying this prayer. This tells us that they could not have been alone with any but with Christ after His ascension. Christ Jesus, His Spirit animating the blood, the one alone with you in the closet showing us *our* Father. His sacrificial blood has gone into the base of the Lampstand, as if we are the priest, helped to bring it into the Holy of Holies smearing the mercy seat and before it. Saving blood from the brazen altar is saving blood from the cross, shed for yours and my eternal life.

Blood from this place is the beginning of all spiritual life. This includes the base of the lampstand, which is here in my heart, the place of the "first things" which we rightly recognize as the *koilia*, the Greek term for the bowels. It is the "eternal life-giving water" the Samaritan woman would have drawn, had she known how to get at the "living water," just below the well water. This fountain, this Rock of Horeb, is indeed the spring of life, like the oil brought up to the flame. We shall consider Matthew 6: 9–12 in more depth later, but for now consider the words of the prophet:

> "Ho! Everyone who thirsts, come to the waters; and you who have no money, come, buy and eat. Yes, come, buy wine and milk without money and without price" (Isaiah 55:1–2).

Was Isaiah speaking of the purchasing power of the faith that welcomes "God's gifts"? He speaks of the most treasured simplicities of life, free to the one who stands upright making a place for the "first things"—"Love the Lord with all your heart."

There in the courtyard of the tabernacle we find the engine of offering, the brazen altar, and the blood of countless helpless animals, their eyes looking out in innocence at their fate in the hands of the ones they have been entrusted to. Clean, unspotted by soil for the unending work of cleansing and covering sin. Without the shedding of blood, there is no remission of sin (Leviticus 17:11). Like the base of the lampstand, Christ is in our hearts, ever serving by His onetime sacrificial gift of cleansing the soul unto eternal life. Mercifully, His blood is applied by the Holy Spirit, from out of our heart, to cleanse the conscience.

82 • THE TABERNACLE

The tabernacle is illustrated here without the outer tent and surrounding courtyard. Try to observe the inner structure, head, torso and lower region-laver and altar, as if it were a person standing with a transparent body, and spiritual furnishings.

Consider this quotation from *The Handbook to Bible Study*[11] on the topic of the Bible:

> "There is no question that this book is difficult to interpret [and] it has baffled many through the centuries. In large measure this has been due to the strange symbolism in this apocalyptic literature. Yet it is the very presence of certain literary features that gives us clues to enable us to decode

the book successfully. One must always operate in Bible study with the assumption that God intends the Book to be understood. Somewhere within it must be materials to help with the difficult parts, since it is self-interpreting."

If we stand the tabernacle up, as a person stands in worship, with the brazen altar in its rightful place in the lower region and the "ark" upon the top of this ancient structure, our worship of God is powerfully enhanced. Clearly the veil is removed from your sight and "eye hath seen" the things that God hath revealed to those who love Him. Can you see with spiritual eyes these literary features, these furnishings associated with a tabernacle? It is very probable that most Christians do not yet know that they are the temples of God. The Temple and all of these spiritual furnishings found in Scripture are *antitypical* of priestly activity that correspond to the application of our ministry efforts today as Christians. God's design of the golden lampstand is our primary *type* of ministry office helping to illuminate Truth, creature to creature, revealed in prophetic interpretation.

As we move away from discussion of the lampstand for now, we move upon the supporting ground of additional helps for the seeker. We may all be pleased to observe what God has proposed for our eyes, and for our ears to see and hear. It was with some interest that you gazed upon your own *tabernacle* on the above page, which God intended for your spiritual identity, that is until you come to know (know ye not?) that you are the temple of the living God. Are you a wandering tabernacle? Visualize your head and the trunk of your body with those furnishings spiritually within: The ark, your head; the menorah, showbread, and golden censer at your chest cavity; laver and brazen altar at the bowels, the seat of human reason and feelings. (See Animated graphic: www.TabernacleHome.com)

You would be a person, by such visual illustration, standing upon your feet in worship, and while you may not embody within yourself these temple furnishings, they are representations of the spiritual offices of the tabernacle and its inner court. As we look upon these symbolic graphics, we shall have an amazing example of a standing temple. There is much to say concerning Scripture, as we consider what the Bible is saying to the church through God's prophetic speech. While we will not cover all the many details, we will cover selected temple offices as spiritual realities from out of the Bible.

As God views this structure, your *head* is actually the "*Ark of the Covenant*"! Step back and take a deep breath; finally the ark has been found, the mystery solved, and all those ark hunters may go home frustrated, not having found the thing and their minds thoroughly blown. I have added some of the interesting Scripture references to these offices, as follows:

TABERNACLE
Spiritual offices

"... a continual burnt offering [throughout] your generations..." —Ex. 29:42

"... And whenever you stand praying..." –Mk 11:25

"... that the men pray in every place, lifting up holy hands..." —1 Tim 2:8

"... They shall mount up with wings like eagles..." —Is. 40:31

The Indwelling Christ

A Minister of the sanctuary and of the true tabernacle which the Lord erected, and not man. —Heb. 8:2

Therefore, brethren, having boldness to enter the Holiest by the blood of Jesus —Heb 10:19

Do you not know that you are the temple of God and that the Spirit of God dwells in you? —1 Co 3:16

In My Father's house are many mansions; if *it were* not *so,* I would have told you. I go to prepare a place for you. —John 14:2

Ark

"... I will put My law in their minds... write it on their hearts ..." —Jer. 31:33b

"And these words which I command . . ." 8b "... they shall be as frontlets between your eyes." —Deut. 6:6,8b

"He has blinded their eyes... Lest they should see with their eyes... Lest they should understand with their hearts . . ." —Jn. 12:40

"Set your mind on things above . . ." —Col. 3:2

"... ark of your strength." Psa. 132:8 "... with all your strength." —Deut. 6:5

"You shall love the Lord... with all your mind." —Matt. 22:37

Lampstand

"He had in His right hand seven stars . . ." —Rev. 1:16

"... The seven stars are the angels of the seven churches." —Rev. 1:20

"The Spirit of the Lord shall rest upon Him, The Spirit of wisdom and understanding, The Spirit of counsel and might, The Spirit of knowledge and of the fear of the Lord." —Isa. 11:2

"... A fountain shall flow from the house of the Lord . . ." —Joel 3:18

"... These things says He who has the seven Spirits of God and the seven stars . . ." —Rev. 3:1

"but whoever drinks of the water that I shall give him will never thirst . . ." —John 4:14

"... 'Upon whom you see the Spirit descending, and remaining on Him, this is He who baptizes with the Holy Spirit.'" —John 1:33

"Thy word is a lamp unto my feet, And light unto my path." —Psalm 119:105

Censer

"... golden bowls full of incense, which are the prayers of the saints." —Rev. 5:8

"and the smoke of the incense, with the prayers of the saints, ascended before God from the angel's hand." —Rev. 8:4

"Aaron shall burn on it sweet incense every morning; when he tends the lamps, he shall burn incense on it." —Ex. 30:6

Shewbread

"And you shall set the Shewbread* on the table before Me always." —Ex. 25:30

"And Jesus said to them, "I am the bread of life." —John 6:35

Cherubim

"... you shall make the cherubim at the two ends of it *of one piece* with the mercy seat. —Ex. 25:19 (NIV)

"... I will meet with you ... from between the two cherubim ... —Ex. 25:22

"So ... to Shiloh ... they might bring from there the ark of the covenant of the Lord of hosts, who dwells *between* the cherubim." —1 Sam. 4:4

Altar

"You shall make an altar." —Ex.27:1

"... The altar shall be most Holy." —Ex. 40:10

---

* Showbread: The bread of presence

"Do you not know yourselves, that Jesus Christ is in you?"
—2 Corth.13:5

"...a priest forever, According to the order of Melchizedek."
—Heb. 5:6

"...the Spirit of Christ who was in them..." —1 Pet. 1:11

"...My Father will love him, and We will come to him and make Our home with him." —Jn. 14:23

LAVER

"...I have put My Spirit upon Him..." —Isa. 42:1

"...the Holy Spirit descended...bodily...like a dove upon Him."
—Luke 3:22

"...strengthened with might through His Spirit in the inner man..." —Eph. 3:16

"...God...has sealed us and given us the Spirit in our hearts..."
—2 Co. 1:21-22

"...But the water that I shall give him will become in him a fountain of water springing up into everlasting life." —John 4:14

...rivers out of the stomach of him will flow of water living. (Grk.)
—Jn. 7:38

Was Moses instructed to place the Ten Commandments in the ark? The obvious answer is yes. If the ark is representative of man's head, including the mind, we find these two interesting relationships, "mind" and "strength." Examples of a strong mind would include remembering the Word of God, or placing the Word as "frontlets between your eyes." "The Word shall be in your heart"—to the Hebrew, the central thing of a man, which would include the mind. Matthew 22:37 records

Christ's phrasing of Deuteronomy 6:5 as substituting the word *mind* for the word strength, either an error and misquote or a cautious road sign, "be prepared to stop!" Subtle yet biblically self-interpreting! David prays in Psalm 132:8 "the ark of Your strength." Mark includes both strength and mind together (Mark 12:30), as he relates what he heard Christ say.

Such variations in Scripture should always be viewed as a challenge to observe more of the facts and look deeper into the truth hidden behind these apparent contradictions-since we know there are no contradictions in the Bible!

Lastly, we will find that the Hebrew word for "*before*" is found many times in our modern versions of the Bible and is translated numerous times as "*face.*"

> "Then you shall place them in the tabernacle of meeting* before the Testimony,** where I meet with you" (Numbers 17:4).

Before, or the *face* of the Ark where Moses had all the leaders in the camp place their staves may here be another self-interpreting aspect of this revelation. Our eye that did not see may be seeing this term "before" translated in the original as "face" 390 times; interesting that the man we superimposed over the tabernacle compound now has a face! Much of Scripture is yet to be revealed, and we are hopeful that our use of the text might enhance interest in these tabernacle furnishings.

---

* Ex. 29:42, 30:36; Num. 17:7
** Ex. 25:16

6

THE TABERNACLE

In order to understand the Bible's deeper truth, as it speaks out of the Old Covenant and into the New Covenant, would it be easier if learners would hear and see spiritual *types* and *antitypes* from out of a new heart. If you are a mature Christian, with your salvation well behind you and your ongoing sanctification, likeness to Christ, and ministerial activities in balance, your understanding should be, in some ways, *more* difficult. Most of those having an older "new heart" have become further removed from the "first things":

> We have much to say, and hard to explain, since you have become dull of hearing. For though by this time you ought to be teachers, you need someone to teach you again the first principles of the oracles of God (Hebrews 5:11–13).

More than often, while we are in our thought life, we may not feel ourselves to be in rebellion against these unmistakable truths, yet I would rather some were babes in Christ, having filled themselves with milk and sitting down to the first taste of real Bible meat.

Revealed text in its print form has always been there for the teachers to teach. According to Joel 2:28, "I will pour out My Spirit on all flesh," and yet many of these "poured out" textual anecdotes remain unrecognized. Our dear trusted pastors and teachers—to their credit and not because of intellectual decline or spiritual dullness—must wait upon the Holy Spirit. He is the one who must open the eyes and ears to the most startling of these illuminations. Understanding the cardinal value of "first things," loving God in Christ first, awakens us to the Holy Spirits prompting that while in oneness with God, praying, we are taken over, inspired. That the remnants of these times spill over into our Bible reading and cause our focus to linger on portions of text, commonly understood one way, yet in the spirit become clearly antiquated, and in need of clarification, and reformation.

A simple and general reference to a temple is a good place for a prophet to start a revival! "Or do you not know that your body is the temple of the Holy Spirit who is in you . . ." (1 Corinthians 6:19)?

Do you not know? Earlier in the introduction we learned, we are not saved by an idea, not saved by an event in history. We are saved by Jesus' blood. Worship of the Hebrew God in a tabernacle or temple required blood, a *type* of sacrifice! The *antitype*, in the life of Christians, is Jesus' blood sacrifice within us, upon our human altar. We are a temple, whether or not we know we are a temple. If we do not know or if we are thinking in error, the challenge is for us to realize reality. Consider:

> Do you not know that you are the temple of God and that the Spirit of God dwells in you? If anyone defiles the temple of God, God will destroy him. For the temple of God is holy, which temple you are (1 Corinthians 3:16–17).

Paul is stating the obvious: "do you not know?" This is clearly a gentleman's exhortation of a factual premise by way of a question with an implied answer —yes, or as my kids would say: Da! If you do not know that you are a temple, you must believe you are something else. Now, of course, we are wrestling with the notion of "temple" versus "tabernacle" and not "temple of the Holy Spirit" over against "temple of God" or any other comparison. While there is much to add in examining these other possibilities, we are not anywhere close to such questions. We are considering the nature of a tabernacle in relation to a temple.

Often it is helpful to ask what the thing is not in order that we might learn more about what it is! A tabernacle is not a permanent place of activity so much as it is a temporary, mobile facility of ministry here on the earth during this dispensation. *Nelson's New Illustrated Dictionary*[12] explains the tabernacle this way: "the tent that served as a place of worship for the nation of Israel during their early history," adding, "This tabernacle was to *replace the temporary tent* that had been pitched outside the camp" (emphasis added).

> Moses... pitched it outside the camp... and called it the tabernacle of meeting... So it was... that all the people rose... and watched Moses until he had gone into the tabernacle. And it came to pass, when Moses entered

the tabernacle, that the pillar of cloud descended and stood at the door of the tabernacle, and the Lord *talked with Moses*. All the people saw the pillar of cloud standing at the tabernacle door . . ."So the Lord spoke to Moses face to face, as a man speaks to his friend" (Exodus 33:7–11).

The above text described the temporary tabernacle of the prophet Moses, the tent that was used by God. Later, we read of the tabernacle that was shown to Moses on the mountain:

"Let them make Me a sanctuary, that I may dwell *among them*. According to all that I show you, that is, the pattern of the tabernacle . . . just so you shall make it" (Exodus 25:8–9).

So we learn a little more about this structure by what we found it not to be. It was not a tabernacle for Moses to be with God, but a tabernacle for all the people. If we were to apply the tabernacle today as one of our houses of worship, we would have many problems unless we were a Jewish fellowship. The tabernacle was a place for a very different form of worship.

Considering what the tabernacle is, what its functions may be, is our next task. Good Bible study will illuminate this spiritual structure, according to this account in Hebrews:

Moses was divinely instructed when he was about to make the tabernacle. For He said, "See that you make all things according to the pattern shown you on the mountain" (Hebrews 8:5).

Kenneth Wuest in his *Word Studies from the Greek New Testament*[13] explains: "[T]he earthly tabernacle gave proof of the fact that there was a real one, the heavenly one where God Himself dwelt, where Messiah officiates as High Priest."

We are finding out many things about our tabernacle. It is not *the real one*, but it does offer a service to God, and within it are all its implements gathered and used in their proper place and function. Dr. Wuest explains for us, "The Aaronic priests performed their priestly rites in the *representation* of the heavenly tabernacle."

Here are some examples of what is said of the tabernacle in the Bible:

1. A house or dwelling-place (Job 5:24)
2. A portable shrine (comp. Acts 19:24)
3. The human body (2 Corinthians 5:1, 4); a tent, as opposed to a permanent dwelling.
4. The sacred tent (Heb. *mishkan*, "the dwelling place"; Exodus 25:9; Hebrews 8:5)

Many more observations can be found in Scripture that will aid us in our understanding of what God was saying and doing with this marvelous structure. You may want to conduct your own research, adding much more to its interpretation and application. To be clear about the tabernacle's purpose, while it was only to be temporary, it was to be the way for people to sacrifice, come to know and to love God.

This was not some human idea of a vehicle to bring an entire race, cleansed in animal blood, into relationship with a Holy God. While people have great ideas and are most creative in their efforts, they do not have the advantages of time, past, present, and future, in their designs. Humanity was not present in the beginning of the design stages of the creatures that they are, or will one day become; therefore we cannot understand all that our Designer intended for the tabernacle's use within His creation.

Because the human body is temporal and God's creature is created with everlasting components called soul and spirit, we are not capable of understanding how these forces are bound to one another—assuming we wanted to enter the creation game and work with these interrelationships. Consider the Herculean task of contemplating the existence of the soul! How does one go about making the first one and causing it to duplicate itself inside the life form of a nearly perfect offspring? Mercifully, we have a God to handle such complex systems.

The tabernacle, as a temporary dwelling place for a priest to conduct the function of making people clean and holy, is a remarkable concept. I think it is safe to say that people would hardly have thought of using such a device. We mentioned the problem of time in relation to understanding how the tabernacle fits into God's plan. It is all very well that we have the Bible to help us get around some of these difficult issues, yet while the Word answers many questions, it poses many more interesting ones as well. A tabernacle's purpose may be threefold, bound up in what it was made for, what it is used for today, and, most important, what it is used for outside of our temporal understanding. Time is an agent and ally for the Christian and more so for the prophetic Christian because of what the Bible tells us will be. As we have noted earlier, Kenneth Wuest reminded us that God said, "According to all that I show you, the pattern of the tabernacle...just so you shall make it" (Exodus 25:9).

There are priests ... who serve the copy and shadow of the heavenly things ... Hebrews 8:4–5).

There is, in other words, another tabernacle. While our interest level should be rising with the discussion of such amazing revelations, our knowledge base will not be able to catch up and stay the course. There are too many mysteries, and the spiritual depths of the tabernacle and the temple are too deep. Its supernatural scope, all the elements that went into the tabernacle and the temple, prevent our natural eyes from beholding these mysteries all at once with perfect certainty. Therefore we must stay close to the shoreline where we shall not sink down and be lost in folly. The Word of God is clear upon the broad and larger issues intended for the times in which we live. The Son has left us His testimony, the Bible, and it will help us come close to God and understand, if only in the shallows, things concerning the tabernacle.

After having described the tabernacle, a sort of *antitype* for the human body, we are now able to view more accurately the furnishings within. It will be helpful to remember that the tent and furnishings are *types* for spiritual realities. These furnishings function by the spiritual will of the inner man or woman.

The spiritual furnishings of evangelism are found in the Holy place. Though they may operate without your knowledge of their arrangement within the tabernacle, it should be understood that by knowing what and where they are and how they work, you will only add more power to these extremely mysterious processes. Becoming more and more skillful in the use of these furnishings will be the result of comparing and using biblical truth in ministry.

As the hand manipulates objects in our world for the various tasks we confront, so does the Holy Spirit function as our hands, as we reach into the spiritual world, by faith, grasping the furnishings available to us within our own tabernacle. Loving God out of the heart with a whole new understanding empowers us. We learn abiding through a *Holy* Christ within, and His blood makes oneness possible. By this abiding relationship, we move upon enemy ground on behalf of the lost and dying.

7

TEMPLE OR TABERNACLE

From the time Moses dictated the tabernacle construction, later to David and Solomon's replacing the tabernacle with the temple, and down to the arrival of Jesus Christ, we have believers walking with God, but without the revelation of what a tabernacle really was. Many Jews wandered in that desert those forty years, and the symbolism was lost to them: Are we wandering for nothing, they might have asked?

> "Whatsoever things were written aforetime were written for our learning, that we through patience and comfort of the scriptures might have hope" (Romans 15:4, KJV).

In their wandering and rebelling, God still reached out and loved them, blessing their descendants by accurately recording their history: "Now all these things happened unto them for ensamples: and they are written for our admonition, upon whom the ends of the world are come" (1 Corinthians 10:11, KJV). But now that we know what God meant, what gift do we give to the God who needs nothing? As we believers stand before the Father, understanding the tabernacle helps us appreciate our own frame, this tent that we inhabit now (1 Corinthians 3:16). Both temple and tabernacle stood as the house of God; we Christians now are the house of God. By understanding both the temple and the tabernacle, we more clearly appreciate our own relationship with God. The setting up and taking down of the tent as the people were following God *anticipated our own efforts to follow Christ and be more like Him.* We fall and then rise up and rebuild. Those who are the persistent lovers of God, like Joshua and David, are those who have connected with this truth and by faith have moved into the promised land of abiding oneness, the true fountain of fellowship and victory.

We who study Scripture have the benefit of knowing both what happened and what will happen. We need to understand that we are designed to be God's permanent temple. Sanctification is the process of the tabernacle being brought to this land of promise. We can cease struggling and simply abide in the grace that Jesus offers. The land that Israel was promised foreshadows the ground we stand on, as if it were the temple mount of service and worship before a holy God. We understand why Israel was promised divinely protected territory. Both promises come with similar conditions. The more we are in God's presence, the more "land" we claim as children of God.

Aaron's rod was placed in the Ark of the Covenant, a symbol of power for mental tasks. A spiritual rod for defending against destructive forces that prey upon the mind would always be a welcome tool if we knew how to use it. We have this sort of power in the mind, and Moses put it in the ark at God's request. This symbolism of the power of the Word of God within sanctified Christians is strong to pull down the walls of doubt and fear. I also know that I can prepare in the morning with the Word of God for battle during my day.

I read the Bible and go into intimate prayer to burn my essence, my incense, before the Lord. Opening my eyes to God's Word each day and turning my praise and worship toward Him are the *first things*. Praising God, a *first things* principle, empowers me to minister to the lost. This is illustrated in the burning of incense in the Holy Place on the golden censer and moving upon the ground of ministerial principles of the *second things*—loving my neighbor as myself.

This formula, "*first things*" and "*second things*," is how God's love is poured out of me to reclaim what is God's. Rightly understanding this relationship not only brings order but also adds sustaining power to the campaign. Lighting the menorah lamps and the use of the "showbread" is how I take action from the spiritual realm unto the natural. When I fail to reach as high as I am able, asking His forgiveness each day is trimming the wicks to burn brighter. That "to be obedient brings blessings" is understood in the blazing light of true righteousness as it illuminates from within outward. My being comes alive in spiritual awareness as I rehearse the Word "hidden in my heart, that I might not sin against You" (Psalm 119:11).

Christ in me by the Holy Spirit is the blessed source of life. Christ in the blood, within my heart, cleansing my soul one time having made me an eternal spirit. I am no more a common soul, fuel for the devil's fire. I am spiritually sealed into a fountain of life bubbling up, the refreshing love of God poured out in sacrifice upon the thirsty land. Jesus has come out of the grave, empowering His messengers with the gift of life (Revelation 1:18).

We must be aware that there is order in the "first things": love God, and the "second things" will follow. "I have this against you, that you have left your first love" (Revelation 2:4). We believers must recognize our first love is glorifying God and making holy His name. More than we can possibly comprehend is the holiness of the name of the Father, yet exactly this we are called to do and will spend eternity doing it. The process of burning oneself before God is a very difficult concept, but easier to understand when one recognizes that all we need do is spend more time making holy His name—putting away the tabernacle and completing the temple building.

Christ's Galilean ministry had displayed many miraculous powers, healing, with preaching among the people. Nevertheless, He was all but driven from His home area (Luke 4:28–29) and did not have much success because of the lack of faith He found in His own hometown. A huge part of their unbelief was that, as Jews, they believed their righteousness was found in keeping the law. They did not believe their sin was dealt with as simply as believing their Savior.

The essential aspect of our spiritual nature is this: "Christ within us. " We, as natural people in this natural realm, use our mental faculties to deal with life issues that confront us daily. We are very good at thinking, yet it must never be the mind alone which connects us to life issues. It is the mind and heart, a harmonious deeper power from out of Christ, in residence, that Spiritually springs up within us. This new life springs from the heart—blood works—to guide, and empower us by the Holy Spirit to learn our lessons in oneness with the Father. Our little mental efforts are magnified, washed in the blood, and all by the power of the Holy Spirit as if our hands burned outward into the lives of our neighbors. We should never want to know ahead of time where such a flame would be used; we must concern ourselves only that our yielded hearts burn with the love of Jesus, asking the lost to accept Christ as Savior and praying for each newfound one.

Will we ever learn to become one with the Father, to focus on God, and then use the Lord's Prayer to prepare us for each day? It is from the heart that outpouring intimate sentiment should flow. The heart must lead the mind into the lost world, while the opposite is true in private praying; the mind leads the heart and sustains elements of intimacy.

Does this sound like the oneness of life that the Holy Spirit speaks of as "the Spirit of Christ" (Romans 8:9) and "the Spirit of [God's] Son" (Galatians 4:6)? This life is appropriated by faith; we merely trust the Holy Spirit to bring us into an abiding oneness with Christ Jesus. At this level of things unseen (Hebrews 11:1), trusting Him is the work of acting upon faith and moving into the spiritual realm. Only when we worship in the spirit (John 4:24) and abide in the Son (1 John 4:12, 16) can we know God's plans, as we first love Him and love the things He loves.

We should understand that a Holy God requires Holy worshippers. Whether you are a tabernacle or a temple is to be realized by recognizing the purpose of these spiritual principles at work within a functioning temple and acting upon them. The one who knows he is a temple is also the one who worships God more faithfully, more consistently—blood sealed and ready to be presented at the court of the Most High.

This is that one, having come down from the mountain, so to speak, filled with the power of proximity with God. We well remember the face of Moses having descended from the Holy Mountain. All who beheld his countenance knew he had come from the presence of the Lord God. Knowing that we have been born from above, and are children of God, helps us understand that a temple must be first, born from God, and then because we come before a Holy God in Jesus' blood, we are born from the *Holy* Christ within (1 John 2:29). His indwelling place is the heart, a *type* first illustrated as the brazen altar found in the courtyard before the tabernacle.

8

BRAZEN ALTAR

Let us consider the significance of the brazen altar as an *antitype* of a place, or a room within Christians. Yes, we have come at last to the place where the *Holy* Christ Jesus is staying. To understand this Holy thing, it may help us to identify it in the terms many Christians throughout the years have used to illustrate its purpose. Often, in evangelism a Christian will refer to the heart or this altar as "a void or a vacuum" which God has created within us. Presumably, those accepting Christ into their lives understand, upon some spiritual level, that Christ Jesus comes into them, into a place God anticipated for His Son's indwelling blood.

With what we have thus far considered, is the Bible teaching that there must be a holy place, a region in the body for Jesus Christ's blood to occupy? It is easy to see why the perception of these Bible truths often created tension in the conversion process. How does one person, Jesus Christ, enter into another person? Christ Jesus entering another lost soul is something we as Christians take for granted while the world stands back and scoffs. I am reminded of the scripture in 1 Corinthians 1:18, "For the message of the cross is foolishness[*] to those who are perishing, but to us who are being saved it is the power of God." We most assuredly can be empowered by the revealed truth found in the teaching upon the tabernacle and thereby become refreshed and persuasive as we speak with our unsaved neighbor.

> "Go therefore and make[**] disciples of all the nations, baptizing them in the name of the Father and of the Son and of the Holy Spirit, teaching them to observe all things that I have commanded you; and lo, I am[***] with you always, *even* to the end of the age" (Matthew 28:19-20).

With these gray lines removed by our present understanding and in their place more descriptive details, we may move through the pages of Scripture without so much skepticism.

It is also true that as our conventional thinking deals with the spiritual implication of these assertions, we will require a bit more evidence to see the details through. In support of the notion of an altar as the place for Holy blood to reside, we should be happy to return again to the Bible and John's first letter for more scriptural guidance, pronouncement, implication, and confirmation.

1 John 2 helps enable our spiritual eyes to see Christ and His blood in relationship to the interior life. We turn back to John's first letter, asking what lies just below the surface.

1 John 2:29 is another *controversial pylon* that opens the

---

[*] 1 Cor. 2:14, 2 Cor. 2:15, [1 Cor. 15:2], Rom. 1:16; 1 Cor. 1:24
[**] Is. 52:10; Luke 24:47
[***] Acts 4:31; 18:10; 23:11

dialogue among commentators and textual experts who must consider whether the last part of this verse is speaking about the *Holy* Christ or God His Father.

We remember 1 John 2:20, which states that "you have an anointing from the *Holy* [one]" and recall that "one" has been erroneously added to the text in many versions. Commentators disagree whether "*Holy* Christ," or "Holy Spirit," is what John is getting at. Is it possible that *Holy* in John's epistle points to Christ, and His dwelling place simultaneously. We shall make our case that the brazen altar is where John is taking us, the most Holy—thing. "... the altar shall be most holy. Whatever touches the altar must be holy (Exodus 29:37).

Again, we are considering the brazen altar as an *antitype* of the human heart—yes, and that place within the lower region where, in Moses' day, blood was sacrificed upon such an altar. A portion of this blood was used to clean things, gaining the Jews acceptable access to God. All of these elements were *types* pointing to their realities, their *antitypes* for the blood of Jesus Christ. You will remember we said earlier, "is the Bible teaching that there must be a holy place, a region in the body for Jesus Christ's blood to occupy? The brazen altar must be that place out of which our prayer begins. For the Christian, everything begins when Christ comes within. It is His interior life that bears the believer, gains him access to the Father.

> "If you know that He is righteous, you know that everyone who practices righteousness is *born of Him*" (1 John 2:29).

Here the highly respected commentator Kenneth Wuest offers this comment:

"Born of God or born of Christ? Nowhere else is it said 'born of Christ.' In the clause 'is born of Him,' the question arises as to whom the pronoun refers, to God or Christ. The context refers the pronoun to the latter [Christ]...Yet nowhere else in Scripture is it said that believers are born of Christ, but always of God."

Another well-respected commentator from Dallas Theological Seminary sees this verse in another way:

> "This verse introduces for the first time in 1 John the explicit thought of new birth. Since the readers *know* that He (God the Father or God the Son) is *righteous*, they would also *know that everyone who does what is right has been born of Him* (the pronoun here probably refers to *God the Father* who regenerates)" [emphasis added].[14]

Henry Alford, in his *New Testament for English Readers*[15], assumes it is Christ to whom John is referring.

The many difficulties commentators have with John's writings should be viewed with great hope rather than bewilderment, doubt, or the fear that Scripture is filled with error. All these fine scholars are nobly hunting for the truth that lies just beyond our understanding. Again, John is speaking to us in the code that has barred unbelievers from God's storehouse for hundreds of years.

To be *born of Him* is to be *smeared* with the blood of a *Holy* Christ moving us, as if by this new birth, into the presence of God. Praying in the Spirit, with all prayer and supplication (see Ephesians 6:18), is without a doubt a spiritual form of the birth from the natural to the spiritual place of the Kingdom of God.

What makes this unique is that we have our transportation into God's presence through Jesus Christ's blood, yet we leave our natural garments in the natural places we pray from. It happens to Christians everywhere all of the time, no matter what you may call it. The problem with those who pray without understanding these tabernacle principles is that there is little spiritual understanding of the phenomenon that is taking place. Therefore, there is less authority to pray, less time devoted to prayer, and just to mention one other lost benefit among many, less power to minister creature to creature.

Consider that while you are praying, you become transported into the place where God resides! Christians in the natural world pass through Christ and His sheep gate into the spiritual world... didn't Christ tell us that His sheep would go "in and out and find pasture"? Is this the birth that Christ spoke about? The woman at the well found that "true worshippers" worship in the spiritual. As if a fountain, spiritual well water, went anywhere but up. All of Scripture attests to this phenomenon with parables, stories, and the greatest miracle beginning with the incarnation, the first birth—a birth from the spirit realm into the natural realm.

What stories can you recall that speak of this theme? Remembering that our eternity begins at conversion helps us see that we may participate, spiritually, in heavenly things. But not with our natural bodies; we must be born again and then birthed, as in 1 John 2:29—born of Christ, into the spiritual realm.

Paul, it may be argued, was fond of the term *raised*, and while his conversation mostly surrounds his teaching with emphasis upon the Word of God, the *logos*, John taught with spiritual emphasis. Peter, another evangelist, focused on the prophetic Word of God with some hints of the spiritual. Peter speaks of "divine nature," a sort of seed or blood reference. He sees the believer moving from the lust of the world to another place; can you see this as spiritual birth? "You may be partakers of the *divine nature*, having *escaped the corruption* (that is) *in the world* through lust" (2 Peter 1:4). Is this birth coming from Christ, not the "born again" (born from above) birth?

"Born of God or born of Christ? Nowhere else is it said 'born of Christ.' Let us consider the assertion in 1 John 2:29 regarding this text, 'everyone who practices righteousness *is born of Him*.'" John is telling us that we are born out of Jesus Christ, out of His blood. Though we may not understand this, Jesus Christ and His shed blood may be one and the same!

> Whoever has been born of God does not sin, for His *seed* remains in him; and he cannot sin, because he has been born of God (1 John 3:9).

"His seed" in the above verse is assumed to be God's seed, which may well be blood from the *Holy* Christ within His believers sealed at salvation. Is this not scientific language for DNA—seed? If the seed remains in a place, is this place the brazen altar?

"[You have] been born again, not of corruptible seed but incorruptible, through the word of God which lives and abides forever" (1 Peter 1:23). Again we find our birth is spoken of in terms of seed in relation to Christ. We should ponder the two characterizations Peter has used in the above verse in relationship to the resurrected Jesus Christ and the indwelling Christ Jesus. Do we understand the deeper implications of the following terms: *lives* and *abides*? *Lives,* suggesting His life is to be lived in God's heavenly kingdom;

Abides, this other term suggesting an "abiding" place, like the brazen altar, as if He will abide within His saints forever. That works well and accords with our understanding of His seed or perhaps blood within us. It also moves us through the text nicely.

After these observations concerning the *born* state of intimate oneness relative to the *Holy* Christ Jesus, it follows that there must be a spiritual place for His seed to reside. The brazen altar answers the need for such a place within the body. Thus we may assume our spiritual birth—abiding oneness—is out of the *Holy* Christ, His blood within the brazen altar. It may be helpful to remember that we are not talking—here—about the Christian's original rebirth that takes place when first we believe. Rather we are talking about being born of Christ ... being born or spiritually raised out of Christ into oneness with God.

We may also learn that this brazen altar is the furnace of the tabernacle complex; all must pass this way, for it is a "most holy" implement, the very heart of the matter.

> He who eats My flesh and drinks My blood abides in Me, and I in him. As the living Father sent Me, and I live because of the Father, so he who feeds on Me will live because of Me (John 6:56–57).

A supernatural phenomenon takes place within this region. Our Father is teaching us an accepted principle by the ancient example of animal sacrifice. We have seen that the place of this sacrifice is in the region of the bowels. We saw the brazen altar illustrated in a man's lower regions. It is no mystery that we are being delicately directed over and into the spiritual understanding of a very simple yet complex collision of two worlds, the physical and the spiritual. The blood sacrifice and burning of animal flesh satisfied the Law in the Old Covenant. There needed to be a clarification in the system, from the "physical" to "spiritual substance."

The numerous applications of innocent blood sacrifice for hundreds of years have illustrated Christ's innocence. Now through illustration and the *types* we've observed, the way was opened, and we were ready for the New Covenant. We could now surrender our souls to Jesus, the spiritual lamb, and receive His blood work once, the sacrifice for sin. The brazen "laver" could now move God's so-loved world over from the physical and into the spiritual world. His work by the Holy Spirit's power, a *type* of priestly duty, the blood cleansing the altar and the bull's blood covering, by sprinkling, on and before the mercy seat. Our faith begins the process of expiation or blood covering, but it is the power of the Holy Spirit that translates the properties of the physical world into the processes that bring heavenward the sacrifice.

Today, it is the blood of Christ that leaves us cleansed, canceling out a temporary bloody tabernacle. This act qualified God's creatures to become the permanent temple by this one-time blood application on the spiritual altar, regardless of additional sin. As Christians, we have learned the value of confessing our sin, recognizing that the brazen laver, a *type* for the place to wash the sins of the day, not only heals the wound but cleanses the conscience.

"He who eats my flesh and drinks my blood," in John 6, was

reported to be a "hard saying" and is for hard evaluation. As natural human regeneration takes place in the region of the bowels, so do these spiritual principles. It's about spiritual regeneration whose beginnings are in the brazen altar, a *type* for the heart. A subtle reference to this region, it may be argued, can be found in the sixth chapter of John's Gospel as he directs our attention into the place where natural flesh and drink are processed, the bowels. Does not our actual blood receive its nourishment in this region? Interesting! It is as if God were wringing us out of our wits, getting our attention; eat Jesus' flesh, drink His blood—are you listening?

Jesus Christ has chosen to move from one creature to another creature on the basis of evangelism and sweet redemption. His love is now made complete in us. We carry His food to others, but only insofar as our feet are washed (John 13:10).

> Herein is our love made perfect, that we may have boldness in the day of judgment: because as he is, so are we in this world (1 John 4:17, KJV).

But only a clean temple makes any offering. If the mind is filled with Scripture and exercised with the praise and worship of God, then we have strength to expel Satan's attacks, whose evil thoughts are meant to sever our oneness. Charles H. Spurgeon wrote, "In my first prayer for deliverance from worldly thoughts, depending on the power and promises of God, for fixing my soul while I prayed, I was helped to enjoy much abstinence from the world for nearly an hour."[16]

When Satan attacks the mind with distracting thoughts, one can ask the Holy Spirit to expel such thoughts or else apply the will, one's own spirit, to expel them in Jesus' name. The dynamic of "God within me, Christ within me," and that place a knowable place, is revolutionary truth, fundamental to Christianity. The point is to accept the reality by faith despite the least practical understanding. His spiritual life living within us is a spiritual phenomenon. While the actual progress of the growth of an individual, with the divine indwelling, takes place in the heart, the process of eating spiritual food and living on the flesh of the Word of God is fundamental.

All Christians have the Holy Spirit, but not all Christians let themselves be taught by the Holy Spirit that by such instruction these principles may become practices.

> I will pray the Father, and He will give you another Helper, that He may abide with you forever—the Spirit of truth, whom the world cannot receive, because it neither sees Him nor knows Him; but you know Him, for He dwells with you and will be in you (John 14:16–17).

The physical picture is clear. Eat physical food and live in the physical. The spiritual interpretation is, "chew on Jesus' words and live in the spiritual." His nourishment is within us, and it is for our use. He is within us by the power of the Holy Spirit.

> "By this we know that He abides in us, by the Spirit whom He has given us" (1 John 3:24).

Our spiritual food is "The bread of us, for being, give to us today" (as the "Lord's prayer" would read, translated word for word from the Greek). Thus, one should stand and pray, if for no other reason, because this spiritual phenomenon will strengthen us to walk each day. A. W. Tozer wrote:

> *A spiritual kingdom lies all about us, enclosing us, embracing us, altogether within reach of our inner selves, waiting for us to recognize it. God Himself is here waiting for our response to His presence. This eternal world will come alive to us the moment we begin to reckon upon its reality.*[17]

Ye are not in the flesh, but in the Spirit, if so be that the Spirit of God dwell in you. Now if any man have not the* *Spirit of Christ*, he is none of his (Romans 8:9, KJV).

Thus, every person who is saved and is indwelt by the Holy Spirit is "in the Spirit." Thus, we are not talking of some method of getting into the Spirit as much as living out the truth that we are already "in." This discussion concerns a *method of realizing* that one is in the Spirit *and the power derived from acting on that fact.* Quench not the Spirit. Despise not prophesying(s). Prove all things; hold fast that which is good. Abstain from all appearance of evil (1 Thessalonians 5:19–22, KJV).

As we are told to not "quench the Spirit," we are also told to not despise *prophesying.* These two go together because the Holy Spirit is the voice of prophecies: they are His words out of the *life* and *speech* of Jesus to His people. Despising His words to us is the best way to quench Him. What has happened to the church today is that there was a shift away from allowing the

---

* Should we assume the flesh (Lev. 17:11) of Acts 2:31 and Psalms 16:10 was that which helps us clarify the above text, the teaching of the indwelling Christ; The blood animated by the "Spirit of Christ."

ones selected by the Holy Spirit to prophesy so that we have remaining only those selected by the Holy Spirit to teach. Our goal should be to use the spiritual resources of the Holy Spirit to both prophesy and teach that we might move the church forward through some rough seas. Praying in the Son to the Father by the power of the Holy Spirit will open some prophetic eyes and thus prophetic speech toward supporting the teaching that is currently happening in the church. God's inhabiting this sort of prayer and praise will strengthen the purpose of Bible teaching in practical ways (1 Thessalonians 5:21–22).

We know that no human can prove what is His plan without God's own power. Therefore, where does one obtain power to both "prove all things" and "abstain from evil"? By spending time each day in close, intimate fellowship in the Spirit with the Son. "Prophetic utterance" is not only vital to the church; it is the very voice of God to us. When John was "in the Spirit" on the Isle of Patmos, he "turned" (Revelation 1:12) and then "fell" (v. 17). He clearly was standing while he was praying. As Francis Schaffer[18] has noted,

> *Christian mysticism is communion with Jesus Christ. It is not 'oneness' with the universe or some other New Age philosophy. The Eastern religious 'mystic' dotes on losing his self so that he is 'one' with all instead of remaining a distinct, unique, responsible free will soul. This would be why he sits and meditates. Jesus wants to give us what He gave us initially: a unique soul with the ability to freely choose.*

Thou, when thou prayest, enter into thy closet, and when thou hast shut thy door, pray to thy Father which is in secret; and thy Father which seeth in secret shall reward thee openly. But when ye pray, use not vain repetitions, as the heathen do: for they think that they shall be heard for their much speaking (Matthew 6:6–7, KJV).

The Buddhist and Hindu are the archetypal "vain repeaters," and prayer wheels and flags are my friend Daniel's favorite example of applying technology to religion. Jesus' command to pray includes His commands on *how* to pray. First: it is in secret. Second: it is with the mind (which includes the will). There is value in group prayers, but each Christian's daily, *primary* prayers should be alone with God. This power to pray and evangelize is out of this seed, Christ Jesus in the brazen altar, and by the Holy Spirit – "The Spirit of the Lord shall rest upon Him" (Isaiah 11:1-2).

"Proverbs 8:34 exclaims, 'Blessed is the man who listens to me, watching daily at my gates, waiting at the posts of my doors.' Notice the word *daily*. We must take deliberate steps each day to bring our minds, bodies, and lives under control so that we can spend time waiting and listening for God to speak."[19]

Company distracts, and we hear other humans long before we hear God, who "is a Spirit: and they that worship him must worship him in spirit and in truth" (John 4:24, KJV). And when we pray, we need to be sure to avoid repeating words instead of doing what the word says: "hallow God's name." We can do this once we learn that speech is but one form of relating the message.

John the Baptist quoted Isaiah, saying, "I am the voice of one crying in the wilderness, Make straight the way for the Lord" (John 1:23). While not exactly "interpretation" of Scripture, these verses have the application of moving us toward God in spiritual unity by a direct route. Thus, spiritual dynamics tend to conserve effort and resources while they tend to maximize spiritual power. God's way is perfect, straight, and these principles direct the reader's attention toward the physical posture of praying. Prayer and praise are not a static pool to contemplate! As we noted earlier, praise from one's own heart can be a course of faith-filled spiritual water that the body was built to channel, whether in a torrent of ecstatic praise or the murmuring stream of serenity.

One finds great tranquility in the God of all circumstances and in the Son. These "rivers" within the believer, says the Lord, are most assuredly supernatural. Consider John 7:38-39:

Christ communicates the Spirit, a thought underlined by John 7:39b. A parallel to the idea of water flowing from a person may be found in the metaphorical rock (i.e. Christ) in 1 Corinthians 10:4. John 7:39 links the coming of the Spirit to the period subsequent to the death, resurrection and ascension of Jesus.[20]

It is interesting that John refers (in 7:38) to "rivers," in the plural, flowing out of the heart, while the differing functions of the Holy Spirit have been earlier suggested (first loving God; second, loving your neighbor); a deeper investigation of "*rivers*" plural, versus "*river*" awaits our investigation.

Jesus speaks of the Spirit ("for *He dwells with* you and *will be in you*"—John 14:17). This Scripture links up well with the passage in Revelation 1:10–20, where Christ is viewed in *the spirit realm*, controlling the seven stars in his right hand, and with

Isaiah's Spirit of the Lord (11:1–5). Does this speak of the same Spirit of the Lord as illuminating the first things, and does the physical Dove that rested upon Christ at His baptism speak of the second things? Jesus' mention of rivers flowing from out of the heart and Isaiah's seven spirits of the Lord are interesting because these spirits were in couplet form: wisdom and understanding, counsel and might, knowledge and fear of the Lord. The rivers illustrated in these couplets as spiritual forces may well be references to the Holy Spirit's dual offices resting upon Christ. We see this in Revelation as Christ holds the seven stars in His right hand.

Of further interest is the fact that the brazen laver, a water container in the tabernacle complex, was more or less above the brazen altar or nearer to the Holy places. If we view the tabernacle complex and visualized its furnishings overlaid with our human form, the laver should be seen *above* the brazen altar.

John reminds us of his spiritual understanding of Christ's control of the church, the Menorah lamps afire as if they were Spiritual couplets within the *hands of men, prefiguring "cloven tongues" of God's Spiritual power upon the affairs of men acted out by our hands within this realm. We remember the cloven tongues of fire resting upon the disciples at Pentecost, or the two wings of the Dove descending upon the Savior's head as He rose up from baptism.

> When the Helper comes, whom I shall send to you from the Father, the Spirit of truth who proceeds from the Father, He will testify of Me (John 15:26).

---

* See illustration on page 186.

He who believes in Me, as the Scripture has said, "out of his heart will flow rivers of living water." This water that John 7:38 describes speaks of how God has opened a way for spiritual intimacy between God's children and a seated and glorified Christ whose work is finished and *whose seed dwells and is active within us.* This gives us a picture of our possible pathway to intimacy and service. Every quest and search for meaning in life is answered in Him, the Son, Christ Jesus. He is the "Wellspring" (1 Corinthians 10:4). His sufficiency requires no other source, provision, or assistance that is not of God. He does not require supplies to be brought up from the rear! Jesus is God, and His water of Life[*] flows out of the brazen altar, for this is God's plan that they may know Him, Christ Jesus!

Scripture cries out for an investigation into the intimacy that has been planned for all time, which, by spiritual revelation, may be the more relevant for our time. Here is the complete fellowship of our spiritual heart, soul, and mind revealed in Scripture. The sheep take their pasture, going *in and out* (John 10:9).

As the spiritual realm contains unseen warfare, the apostle Paul reminds us to *stand* with Him (Ephesians 6). We need to maintain our focus up and into this unseen place where we are to "Watch and pray," as Jesus commands us (Matthew 26:41).

---

[*] Is. 12:3; [John 6:35]; Rev. 21:6; 22:17

9

ARK OF THE COVENANT

Inside the Holy of Holies we find one of the more holy implements, the *Ark of the Covenant*. The ark was a wood box overlaid with hammered gold. This vehicle was, among other things, the adjudicator which moved the people through time and space. Power and truth from the spirit world was often manifest through the application of its mysteries into the physical world. If you would take the time to research Moses' experiences throughout his exilic campaigns, or Joshua, David and others whose efforts were magnified by God through this instrument, you would agree, this was not an ordinary box resting within the Holy of Holies.

The most Holy "place" in the tabernacle structure was the Holy of Holies, also called the most holy place, where God would "meet with you between the two cherubim." There I will meet with you, and I will speak with you from above the mercy seat, from between the two cherubim which are on the ark of the Testimony (Exodus 25:22).

It should be pointed out that the holiest *article* of this tabernacle is the brazen altar, not the ark of the covenant. This helps us see how God has placed importance upon His Son's work. The symbolism of the seemingly endless stream of innocent animals slaughtered for blood sacrifice is sorrowful. Ceremonially, this blood was offered to pay for sin, and clean the conscience of men throughout some fifteen hundred years. Jesus Christ allowed Himself to be placed upon the cross and is become an *antitype* for all those slaughtered animals. (Isaiah 53:6).

Atop the ark is the mercy seat, with two cherubim, one piece of hammered out gold.

> The cherubim shall stretch forth their wings on high, covering the mercy seat with their wings, and their faces shall look one to another; toward the mercy seat shall the faces of the cherubim be (Exodus 25:20, NKJV).

When we learn to conceptualize "sprinkled blood" upon the mercy seat, as was done for priestly atonement, and the sins of the people, we see God is here speaking out of these events by repetition the deepest *type* of meaning. For some fifteen hundred years, blood was sprinkled atop this ark's mercy seat because of sin. What's going on here? Well, I need to remind you that the top of your head forms an *antitype*—for the lid of the ark of the covenant. Keep breathing…slowly go back and re-read that last phrase and breath!

The mercy seat, the lid atop the ark is a *type* God had shown Moses to teach His children Holiness, and forgiveness so that they might come near to Him. What does that have to do with the top of my head? Hmm, it does get more interesting!

Remember that this lid had two cherubim on its ends. The world over, we see contemporary Christians at worship in the churches of our day, raising their hands toward heaven unto God. These raised hands symbolize Holy Spiritual power and are *antitypes* of the cherubim associated with the lid of the ark, or the mercy seat. I mean, "you didn't know this"? Now just stay with me here for a minute!

Arguably, Jesus' actual blood is *spiritually smeared* upon a Christians head. This substance is unlike anything else within this creation, unlike anything we know or have experienced outside of a new, clean heart. Aside from eternally saving Christians, it cleanses the conscience and is the first thing God sees when we come before Him. Yes, Moses directed the first sprinkling upon the mercy seat, and that seven times (a perfect Jewish number) for complete covering, a *type*. This is where God said He would meet with them, between the two cherubim. Are you still there?

The priest within your body (you, dear friend), the new man, offers up this sprinkling, and it is actuated by the Holy Spirit. Whether a continuous phenomenon or an involuntary rendering upon each interface with God, I do not know. These are the things of the Spirit of God. We call this miracle propitiation by atonement, and its eventual result is "abiding oneness"! Again, how it happens is a spiritual mystery and a wondrous phenomenon of the glory of God.

The wings of the two cherubim, while they cover the mercy seat in symbolic *type*, participate in holy vitality. When we see today's application of the wings, we see outstretched hands praising God, *antitypes*. The Hebrew writer identifies these two ministering hands as "heavenly things" (Hebrews 9:23-24) purified with better sacrifices (plural—for daily sacrificial prayers).

Ironically, Egyptian gold forming the pairs was hammered out from one piece of solid stock, the cherubim one (piece) with the lid, even as we find that our hands are connected to our arms, shoulders, neck, and head in one piece through the body.

Christ, we might observe, was a perfect and excellent minister by *types* as if His two hands—His disciples—were sent out by twos (Mark 6:7). We also minister, whether by our own two hands reaching into heaven or these hands, *antitype* ministers searching out the lost. We who have the Holy Spirit, these *types* of cherubim upon the mercy seat, can pierce the supernatural boundaries awaiting the birth of private prayer.

Inside the ark and under the mercy seat, the staff, the manna, and the tablets of law show the connection between the Old and New Covenants. The word is on the tablets, the power of God is in the staff, and the bread (manna) that feeds us (John 6:35, 48) is a reminder of Jesus' love and His faithfulness for us while supplying all our needs, both physical and spiritual. Jesus is the Word of God (John 1:1–3). The sample of manna that miraculously provided for the Israelites reminds us that the same loving God miraculously provides for us now in whatever He asks us to do. "Aaron's rod that budded" mirrors the staff Moses held, and which he held aloft in victory (see Exodus 17:9, 11, 14). The strength of the mind can be seen as an *antitype* symbolized by this rod, and it reminds us of our access to God's power, the power of the mind available to do what He gives us to do; "you ... be strengthened with might ... in the inner man" (Ephesians 3:16). This power of ours is like the things we bring along, *types* of fishes and loaves—our part in the miracle of ministry. His part is always multiplication in supernatural power.

The reality of the tabernacle is that it is the vehicle by which man attempts to make his connection with God. Israel had the earthly tabernacle, and yet they were a rebellious people. Forty years they wandered in a barren desert, seemingly lost, yet always under God's care. Forty years, essentially, they lived with God, yet their bodies fell in the desert, condemned. We see ourselves in this as we struggle to know God more intimately. We struggle with that same wandering, from the gates of Egypt all the way into the Promised Land. The Israelites were being drawn into that Promised Land, but they were rebellious. They didn't understand that God is a jealous God desiring their sacrifice, worship, and praise.

According to the Bible, God alone is to be worshiped or served (Ex. 20:1–3). He is to be served with man's whole being (Dt. 6:5; Lk. 10:27). Mind as well as emotions, physique as well as feelings are to combine in God's praise.[21]

The Israelites, under Moses' leadership, didn't get it. Most of these people died never having reached their Promised Land. The relationship between Jesus Christ and the tabernacle has been the subject of many books. We see His sacrificial work in the brazen altar. Numbers 19:2–4 describes the necessary sacrifice of the red heifer outside the city, the blood then brought into the camp before the tabernacle. Jesus was sacrificed on Golgotha outside the city, and His death there resulted in His blood being brought into Israel as His blood is brought into our hearts. It is as if God chose a name for Israel in the name Jacob that we might understand that the *Holy* blood was brought into Jacob, into a man, into mankind.

We also see the significance of His suffering and His death, His blood fulfilling the entire sacrificial system, solving by this blood each circumstance in one's life, from the least to the greatest. By His *Holy* blood, a Holy God becomes our Father; born by the Holy Spirit, we can praise "our" Father. The lessons of the tabernacle are many. Can we learn these few basics of intimacy with God and efficacy with our neighbors? We all are moving from the tabernacle to "know ye not that your body is the temple...of God?" (1 Corinthians 6:19).

As we said earlier, the Israelites were being drawn into that Promised Land, but they were rebellious. Will you be one who understands the significance of these amazing lessons? Israel didn't understand that God is a jealous God desiring sacrifice. Stand up and look into the Name of God. He awaits you between the two cherubim; worship and praise him. Lift up your eyes; your strength is your spiritual gaze into the Father. It is a short walk over onto the real Promised Land!

Well and good that we have found ourselves upon Holy ground and have understood through the eyes of prophetic inspiration these observations of the furnishings such as the ark, menorah, brazen laver, and brazen altar. These truths are truly wonders to behold, and if we are inclined to spend more time in evaluation, exploration, and deeper investigation of these discoveries, no one should blame us. Yet these few mysteries pale in significance as only individual episodes upon the stage of their purpose in the great masterpiece of the Godhead, the spiritual plan for human redemption and sanctification.

Remember that it is God who loves you. God has always loved you, and He wants to hear from you every moment of the day. For that is what true love does it loves. What we have talked about here and before is only about the instruments He has created for loving us. God awaits your expressions, the voice of your heart, creature to Creator.

Having discussed the means to reach into heaven—the hardware—so to speak, we should move along and discuss the installation of the software.

He has opened the Scripture for each day, for our sure reading and understanding the things He loves us to hear, His Word. He is now showing us how He wants us to come to Him from out of a more contemporary understanding of His Word. There are no fuzzy lines or obscured suggestions of what Christians should say to God and what the Son has proclaimed for our fellowship with Him.

Without Christ, the world has no standing to communicate with God. We as Christians are told clearly in the Word what we should say. He tells us to *hallow* His name and the times for these occasions. Remember Aaron and the priests lit the lamps—first thing every morning—and burned their incense before the Lord (Exodus 30:7), and reminded us of the *types* of sacrifice, blood sacrifice every morning throughout your generations (Exodus 29:42). So let us evaluate the substance of our spiritual expressions remembering that they are *types*, and having looked deeply at their instrumentation, we turn to the speech of the heart.

We know that the Scripture is largely silent concerning the *mechanics*, *methods*, and *content* of desired intimacy in prayer. We have only the teachings upon the Lord's prayer, and the observations of Jesus alone in prayer. At least two things can be deduced from this silence:

(1) Because of the great importance of communion with God, His silence upon the subject must be understood to cause our focus to intensify upon what is written, the Lords prayer.

(2) We should tear apart in reckless abandon that which is left to us. We should search high and low, back through

Scripture, back into our church history to observe and understand the interpretations brought to bear upon the little text we do have. Remembering, we are not looking to rewrite the Bible but to understand prayer, to search out godly men, training our prophets to hear from on high for His inspiration and assistance!

10

DISCIPLE'S PRAYER

The Lord's Prayer In Worship

After this manner therefore pray ye: Our Father whichart in heaven, Hallowed be thy name. Thy kingdomcome. Thy will be done in earth, as it is in heaven. Give us this day our daily bread. And forgive us our debts, as we forgive our debtors. And lead us not into temptation, but deliver us from evil (Matthew 6:9–13, KJV).

After this manner therefore pray ye." John taught his disciples to pray, so Christ's disciples, some of whom were John's disciples, asked Him in Luke 11:1, "Teacher, teach us how to pray." Matthew reports that Jesus prefaced this model prayer with a warning, "When ye pray, use not vain repetitions, as the heathen do: for they think that they shall be heard for their much speaking" (Matthew 6:7, KJV). One of His points concerned the use of "words" in prayer. As Oswald Chambers pointed out, "We have to keep our mouths shut and our spirits alert. God wants to instruct us in regard to His Son, He wants to turn our times of prayer into mounts of transfiguration, and we will not let Him."[22]

What will you "do" with Me as you come in to Me by this prayer? This is what God might be asking us! Does God want to hear out of your heart? When you pray this prayer, are you thinking words because someone taught you thus? Are you in the mental realm, thinking thoughts as if your thought life expressions were new and absorbing to God. Friend, God is not looking for an intellectual encounter with us. Remember, this prayer is not intercessory, or supplication for our needs or the needs of others. Holy God's name, that is what the Bible is teaching us. Matt. 6:9-13 You have come before God, your Father, choosing to fellowship from out of your heart—upward in praise and worship. It is best to remember, you are in the midst of a spiritual column of praise culminating in worship at His feet. A column, or *type* of edifice for burning *up* the substance of a sacrificial offering.

FIRST THINGS

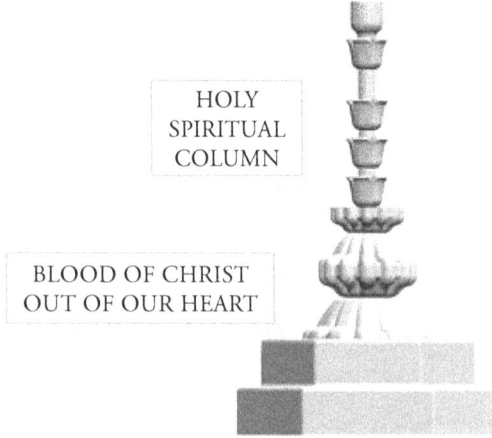

HOLY SPIRITUAL COLUMN

BLOOD OF CHRIST OUT OF OUR HEART

Luke 11:2 tells us that Jesus says, *lego*, "say"; Matthew 6:9 tells us that Jesus says, *houto*, "thus," or pray "like this." While appearing to be a contradiction, this is not so. As you dig deeper into what is actually being said, you make many discoveries, chief among them that the Bible contains not contradictions but for the faithful, a means to deeper clarification. Matthew's account actually says *houto oun*, "thus therefore," or "this way for this reason." Luke's account omits the reasons, and we must remember that Jesus instructed His disciples on more than one occasion in this discipline of private prayer. Luke's account seems to omit "our" in just about every Bible version including the Greek, except in the King James and New King James Version. We should not be too concerned with this phrasing in Luke, as *Father* is clearly the point.

It seems we can agree these Gospel writers were suggesting that this prayer is a model—or that prayer is best done while it is left intact as a model. Such words of authority and power from Christ's lips deserve deep consideration, and they will always be vital.

The ability to focus in oneness while praying is difficult enough without allowing the freedom of the mind to express itself along with the contaminating fiery darts of an enemy, which may have access to the thought life. Pray within this structure because it is all that you are able to do while you are at war in the spiritual realm of hallowing, or separating God's name from little gods! You're the new spiritual creature out there barely, to an age of seventy-five or eighty-odd years old; that's why He has written to you! That's why His prayer to you is easy to know and hard to do as a "streaming" peace offering. There may be many evil spirits out there opposing you, and they've been doing so for millennia.

Your focus should be upon two things here, the name of God and His place above you. Prayer that begins in the brazen altar is empowered prayer, having the onetime sealing of the sacrificial atonement. It should be enough for you to be mindful of these two facts: "focus on God" from within Christ, while you are "hallowing His Name."

I think this is what Christ was getting at; this is what Luke was hearing Christ to mean. It is difficult to focus upon the name of God! Our troubles begin when we allow our minds too much freedom of expression while in this prayer. Just as a good sermon has three points to remember, this prayer has a track to follow, helping us stay safely on the road. Spiritual oneness is difficult to maintain, and to focus on God's name is even more difficult while adding improvisation, a recipe for failure. Loving God in Christ while in this model spiritually allows a great deal of creature-to-Creator expression. Most of the Lord's prayer, especially when focus is upon the first part, should be about loving God! Hallowing God's name proficiently becomes an amazing anticipated practice!

> "From the rising of the sun, even to its going down, My name shall be great among the Gentiles; In every place incense shall be offered to My name, And a pure offering; For My name shall be great among the nations," Says the Lord of hosts (Malachi 1:11).

What we learn from Malachi's prophecy concerns incense burning everywhere, every minute around the world. Since the Christian Gentile does not burn physical incense everywhere the sun shines, it appears we must come over to the spiritual side of understanding the text. Private prayer and the burning of the Lord's prayer, a kind of incense, out of my heart is concerned with a *holy* ancient task of a *peace* offering to God. This sounds very much like our desire to *thank, vow,* and *love* God consciously by understanding the Old Covenant and applying blood upon the altar of our hearts. "I will freely sacrifice to You; I will praise Your name, O Lord, for it is good" (Psalm 54:6).

One of the great mysteries of the Bible is the great love affair that went on for about fifty days when Christ came and breathed into the disciples in the upper room (John 20:22). Where are the volumes of sentiment and joyous memories that were experienced between the apostles, Christ, and our Father? Christ chose not to have the volumes written, having its occasions far too intimate for our rude eyes and ears. There remains no record of those amazing love stories!

"When He had said this, He breathed on them . . ." These men received Jesus' blood into them, which marked one of the greatest events in history. It is found in the above often-overlooked verse. You will recall in verse 21, Christ moves into the room with the salutation, "Peace to you! As the Father has sent Me, I also send you," which subsequent sending does not happen for two months, curious!

Why do we not talk about this lag in commissioning on behalf of the lost? The preachers and teachers of our day would never begin a campaign to save the lost on Sunday morning and wait to implement the action two months later. Where is the momentum, the power of the challenge from the pulpit to "go out"? Has it slipped away, or should we listen with spiritual ears to Christ who has told us to go today while waiting months until we go out tomorrow? That is just the way our Savior likes to work: He speaks the words so we hear them in amazing ways.

If we revisit His statements in chapter 20, "sending" seems to be the topic, while "filling" us up is the activity that is taking place. We have now set aside His "sending" us and are focused upon the "filling." He breathed on, or in them and said, "Receive." It was never a problem for these men to understand what was happening to them, because Jesus came into them, and they felt His presence, His "blood," with the substance of the breath of life. It must have been a powerful moment in time! While He left within them blood, we should remember, such blood is alive by His God nature, made alive by the power of the Holy Spirit, and known to them by this same will. "His soul was not left in Hades, nor did His flesh see corruption" (Acts 2:31).

These men will not remember Christ telling them, "As the Father has sent Me, I also send you," for many days to come. They are consumed with the joy of life in Christ within them beyond anything we could ever imagine.

When the Holy Spirit opens our eyes, the eyes that did not see, His veil is removed, and the light of understanding falls upon us. Here we are told that before we are to move upon the plain of battle, taking enemy ground, power must be added to our efforts, and power from above will do nicely. Jesus is saying to them, "Receive the Holy Spirit for sealing of Myself within you, to come to Me daily." So they came to this place together and, by ones, came into Jesus separately. Theirs was the first experience of oneness with the Father and that for about two months before the assault upon the spiritual forces of wickedness began.

Notice that John separates the first great event, "breathed on them," from the second event, "receive the Holy Spirit," with the conjunction *and*. Observe the text from John 20:22: "He breathed on them, *and* said to them, 'Receive the Holy Spirit.'" This Holy Spirit filling was for another service over against that of Pentecost. Pentecost was about the ministry He first spoke of. Pentecost is loving our neighbor, a "second things" activity the Holy Spirit will empower 50 days later. The upper room filling was for the administration of first things, "I have this against you, that you have left your "first love'" (Revelation 2:4).

This first love encounter only the disciples experienced and then spent their lives trying to explain it to others. Some of these others, with whom the disciples shared the life, understood their meaning, yet they were later to be accused of leaving "their" first love. When Matthew and Luke tell us to "say" or pray "like this," it is all about what will best support the trance-like state of looking long into the spiritual name of the one you most love, really love, are blown away to be with. Trance is best understood as the one being "in the spirit." "I was in the Spirit on the Lord's Day" (Revelation 1:10a).

Jesus reminds us every morning that as we come to Him, *I will take you to the Father's house for proximity with Him. I have told you that His reward is with Him, and by such proximity there is strength that you will be carried in the day. Just come into my prayer life by the Spirit.* We have the biblical witness of the events of the first things, love God with all your heart. Lest you forget, I will give you another day to get this right.

Such interpretation of Scripture must include the powerful testimony of the Holy Spirit with whom these men were intimately acquainted. It was through His ministry that "all things" came back to their remembrance. It is this power that enables us to experience intimacy on the Spirit level for the first things of knowing God in Christ Jesus. The Holy Spirit's ministry is that which mysteriously makes us one with the blood of Jesus, so that we might not be like the thief or the robber who tries to climb up another way.

> Most assuredly, I say to you, he who does not enter the sheepfold by the door, but climbs up some other way, the same is a thief and a robber (John 10:1).

Jesus Christ is "the way, the truth, and the life." Christ is a door, and because Christ Jesus is in you, sealed in you by His actual blood, your prayers must go through this door. Though the mind conceives by its commitment to a mission to carry such prayer to the Father, the mystery is that it is the priest that is you, dear friend, who must go down to this door by way of the well. Very mysterious speech, yet only this: you must become one with Christ in order to be one with the Father.

We are like the Samaritan woman who tried to get her mind around living water and well water just above the living water. We learn that living water is best brought up and out to be of any use (John 4:10–24). Jesus gave us a simple illustration of lowering our bucket, as if it were a spiritual task of the mind, so to speak.

Jesus directs the Holy Spirit to move your heart praise further on to the Father in the first things, loving God. Our goal is not to focus on the heart to remain in Christ's *dwelling place*—which again is not what we aim at. The Eastern cult or "New Age" contemplation groups seek out truth, absent of Christ's presence, here as an end. No; we enter through the sheep gate to be born in oneness with the *Holy* Christ. We bring into this union our little, and the Holy Spirit makes much of it!

Remembering that you are praying focused upward, tasked with hallowing God's name.

The truth of the *sheep gate* is a great concept that has little value while it remains in the abstract. Once we see in this illustration the spiritual truth of a *Holy* Christ in our heart, we become strong and able to apply by faith abiding oneness. Here is where the strength of oneness translates into love and is added to the business of loving our neighbor.

To pray for your friends and family, church, bishop, pastor, and missionary should be an exercise out of the heart. Power is proximity with God; it is sustained through abiding with God in Christ. The maintenance of this power is a function of a Christ-centered mission coordinated through an active and persistent mind. From these spiritual processes, our physical voices call for the lost in proclamation of the Gospel or the good news and the loving touch of our *Holy* hands.

While your heart seeks to love God as a "first things" principle, the mind leads out in defense of the heart's purpose. While praying for comfort and strength for the needs of others in supplication, we understand this to be a mindful occupation and as such the "second things" of the heart.

Continuing with the Lord's prayer, we shall now look deeper into the Bible for support as we focus upon the heart and its occupation.

11

OUR

The deeper interpretation of "Our," in the beginning of the sixth chapter of Matthew's recorded prayer, is taking on added interest considering all we have learned thus far. In Matthew 6:6, you are told to *go into your quiet room* and be alone. Jesus Christ tells us to say "our," while alone! Does this statement argue strongly for the interpretation that Christ is the only other one with you in that room? Having learned earlier that Christ Jesus is actually within you, the "our" takes on the amazing truth of God's plan, "Christ actually affirming that He is in you," and alone, the two of you at work in the interior place.

Though the prayer, says Augustine, is "*fraternal*," we must remember Christ is also a part of the fraternity and arguably its president. The context of these statements, you will recall, is teaching what not to do. Christ tells the disciples not to use many words and not to use the same words over and over again When you pray, do not use vain repetitions as the heathen do. For they think that they will be heard for their many words. Therefore do not be like them. For your Father knows the things you have need of before you ask Him. In this manner, therefore, pray: Our Father in heaven, Hallowed be Your name (Matthew 6:7–9).

While Jesus teaches one thing, is He also teaching the principle that the disciples are not alone? If we look at the text closely, we may see Jesus' subtle implication. Doesn't He correct them by saying, "Go into your closet and be alone"? Yet His choice of words suggests more than one person in the closet. He says, "Father of us" in verse 9! The "us" is personal, the Greek has it: first person, plural, and genitive; which tells us in simple language, all of "us." All of those who are here receiving this teaching have the same Father. What is the application of these teaching elements if not that each one hearing His voice may be alone with the *Holy* Christ in priestly private prayer to God? *None* of the others may be alone with each other in quite the same way.

In consideration of whether *our* should include Christ: We know of many references in the Bible that Christ uses that refer to Himself as having the Father also?

> "That they all may be one; as thou, Father, art in me, and I in thee" (John 17:21, KJV)

> "Father, if it is Your will, take this cup away from Me" (Luke 22:42).

Is not the speaker at any event also a qualified participant of that event? If so, wasn't Christ there among the other sons of God, thus qualified as one "of us"? Jesus' multilayered speech "our" included His disciples, and His speech included you. He was also speaking to me, and all of us come alone to be with Him through the agency of the Holy Spirit.

He has gathered us together, yet He recommends we come alone in Him, while, by a single poetic translation in the King James version, "our" hints at the notion of oneness. Surely a supernatural phenomenon is being transacted in the closets or private rooms in every country in the world at the same time. The overriding reality of Christ Jesus our Lord is His presence and residence within the believer. *Meno—I in you*—a place fixed and knowable within believers.

> *The presence of the Lord Jesus Christ is the secret of the Christian's strength and joy. You ask me, How can that be? And my answer is, Because Christ is God, and because Christ, after having been made man, went up into the throne and the life of God. And now that blessed Christ Jesus . . . can be in me and can be with me all the days.* —Andrew Murray[23]

Christ stood before these men and taught them to say "Our Father," knowing that, by application, we will each be alone in our closet, uniting ourselves within the heart. We are joined in oneness to the Spirit of Jesus Christ dwelling in us. The Holy Spirit has placed Christ in me one time, placed Christ Jesus into every believer one time, the blood sufficient to cleanse that believer of all sins past, present, and future and regenerate that believer in the inmost heart—one time. He is come within, and His coming is mysteriously holy with power in His right hand to help (Revelation 1:16, 20). With Him we interact in the power of the Holy Spirit to love the Father, to love the lost, and to become more like Himself.

> Now hope does not disappoint, because the love of God has been poured out in our hearts by the Holy Spirit who was given to us (Romans 5:5).

He tells us we're to be alone in our closet (Matthew 6:6), yet He tells us to say, "Our Father." Again, if I'm in my closet by myself, who are the other people—the others "of us"—in this closet? As physical creatures created for both physical and spiritual existence, we need to further examine the supernatural nature of this spiritual truth. This is what our faith is about—the life and times of the amazing and the supernatural. After all is argued, offered up both pro and con, the reality is that Peter walked on water, Peter and Paul both raised the dead in God's power, and John the beloved disciple of Jesus was transported into heaven and returned to the Isle of Patmos.

Once redemption has taken place, the "new man" continues to resides in a physical body. There he chooses to be alone in the closet, and at once he is able to connect with the *indwelling* supernatural presence of Christ Jesus. It is this spiritual reality that we are considering. We have concluded that "our" joins me, joins you to Christ within us, and all of this quite knowable by the Holy Spirit's efforts. God is nudging us over to the spiritual side to understand His words, and once there, we more easily recognize Christ's Spirit speaking from within us.

Thus, if I am in my closet by myself, praying, I am not alone. Here in my room, the *Holy* Christ is in me, and God's Holy Spirit is in me and may be with me. Such biblical truth assumes a connection in the spiritual realm that is beyond my natural comprehension. That Jesus tells us to say "our" only means that our job is to recognize by faith the interior life of

Christ Jesus our Lord. We know that He was speaking to the disciples both in the short term as He walked with them and in the long term, knowing they would live out their lives and be martyred. (The exception was to be the apostle John.) The disciples may also have known that their words would transcend their time and be the substance of our faith in our time.

These men, the apostles, share a unique relationship with Jesus, for His presence was with them physically as they walked with Him, and His presence was later in each of them simultaneously in the upper room (see John 20:22). Also, earlier in that room, they would have heard Him pray to the Father (John 17:11, KJV), "Keep through thine own name those whom thou hast given me, that they may be one, as we are." Later, after Jesus Christ ascended to heaven, they would be able to understand Jesus' very words in the very way He said them: "I am no longer in the world." When they looked up at Him ascending, they truly knew He was God and man risen, His work complete! The blood of Christ within them completed the work of propitiation, opening a way to the Father, as well as opening a way for the Gentile world, for such as you, myself, family and friends.

The application of this great truth moves outward in the love of this supernatural phenomenon, for it is Jesus' blood, accepted by faith in each generation, creature to creature by Holy spiritual evangelism, until His blood arrives in our hearts in this twenty-first century. We are the ones who have received Him, sprinkled with the blood and gladly chained to His original body. Those who have gone on before us are in the great family of Christ, the one who knew no sin and died for our sin that we might live through Him.

To broaden this application in the realm of supplication and intercessory prayer, "our," the first movement in this prayer, is the joy of knowing that around the planet and across time others are also praying to the same Father. These are people whom we will have the privilege of spending eternity getting to know, in a place the Bible calls heaven and the new earth. When we pray, we should have this perspective that we are a part of the body of Christ,* the church that exists across space and time, which is on the move to a place of biblical proportions.

Since the first word in Jesus' model prayer-*our*-is plural, some may interpret this to mean others, thus including all the church. It is easy to forget that God requires sacrifice of each of us, and because loving God has been commanded** by our Lord, it is a "first things" principle. It must be included in our interpretation that "our" does not mean that we are instructed to sacrifice upon the altar for others. This is a personal task and privilege for each one, and it is a private, individual task of ministry. Because we do not know the true condition of another's soul in Christ, we are not to be expected to presume their holiness before God's throne. We come alone in the blood of Christ with our sacrifice of time, treasure, and the truth of the Word. This would be one reason why we get alone with Christ Jesus and the Father—there is private work ahead.

Certainly there is also a place and time for intercessory prayer (and corporate prayer) for the Christian in China, for the Christian in Sudan or Indonesia or Egypt, for the missionary in a foreign land, learning a foreign tongue, ministering to refugees driven from their own country.

---

* Romans 12:5, 1 Corinthians 12:12 "…One body…"
** Matthew 22:37–38: "Jesus said, '"You shall love the Lord your God . . . ' This is the first and great commandment.'"

The interpretation of "our," the first word in this learned prayer, is about relational intimacy with the Father through the Son and by the Holy Spirit. Once this heart has practiced the "first things," loving God, the second things seem to follow with might and persistence. We are commanded to love our neighbor and this should be a byproduct of loving God first, which is the ministration of the outward flow of God's love through us, because we have hope, God's tears become our tears, and our petitions.

> "Rejoice with them that do rejoice, and weep with them that weep" (Romans 12:15).

12

OUR "FATHER"

Jesus Christ has a relationship with the Father unlike our relationship with the Father. J. Vernon McGee once said, "the Lord's prayer (Our Father) is the one prayer that Christ cannot pray. I agree, Jesus Christ did not intend "forgive... (me my)... debts," for Jesus was and is sinless! Christians should agree upon that point. The Bible teaches that Christ is in us and that we are in Christ. His relationship to the Father is vastly different in ways I am unable to understand while in this body, yet Jesus and I do have the same Father. Jesus' blood atoning for my sin, the Holy Spirit within me, my presenter at court, allows for *access* (*prosago*) to Jesus' Father and "our" Father (*Access*—Romans 5:2; Ephesians 2:18; 3:12).

Because it is a fact that we "little born ones" are sealed and saved by Jesus' blood, it makes little difference to our eternal security whether we understand *all* the ways that God is *our* Father. The following far-reaching principle is what I do: I come with Christ Jesus to our Father, and Christ leads out from behind my faith! Abiding oneness with our Father requires faith and makes possible the prayer Jesus Christ encouraged us all to pray.

Jesus Christ taught this prayer to His disciples, and we listen as Bible readers, to what they said two thousand years ago. We know that Jesus Christ has prayed that everyone who listens to the disciples will be kept in the name of the Father. The power of this principle is that God the Father's name is available to us through God the Son, and the Son understands what the Father wants because theirs is the first instance of oneness, making our oneness possible. Christ gives us the understanding that when we come to pray, we understand that abiding oneness with the Son is oneness with the Father.

"Our Father," for each person saved, is the most important subject of the prayer. God is the Father, always has been, always will be. But through Jesus' sacrifice, God is our Father. One can spend a long time dwelling on this fact alone. Once I know God the Father is mine, I then know that He is my Father. He is the one responsible for my existence, my care, and even my salvation.

I also know that He is my disciplinarian and judge when I obey or disobey. But as my Father, He is the one I want to please. And pleasing Him isn't difficult.

> *God wants you alone sometimes because He wants your absolute, undivided attention. What a compliment! A King wants to spend time with you? You get to have an audience with royalty? And He listens to you? And though He is King, He allows you to address Him as Father? Why would you want to do that quickly or with a bunch of background noise? Suppose you might miss what He is saying? Surely, you need to be alone with Him.*[24]

Largely, in early twenty-first-century American culture, it amounts to spending time listening to Him and saying no to many other things like TV, paperbacks, and movies. And since He is my Father, He never stops being my Father, even if I do wander off with those who dislike My Father! When I realize what I've done and return to Him, He is still my Father, I am still His child, and He still loves me. His arms are open to receive me.

Almost every religion acknowledges the Father as God Himself, but that never means that a disbeliever in Jesus Christ who was taught this prayer can pray it. This theme of "Father in heaven" and "His name" is awesome when we as believers have Christ in us, sealed by the power of the Holy Spirit. We become new creatures and have this right to be in a relationship with the Creator.

To be able to relate to this great and vast God, we sometimes use the term *Abba*. Certainly God is awesome. He is fearsome, and yet He wants us to feel secure with Him. He is our Father. We have the access to Him that a child has because of Christ Jesus' work in us by the Holy Spirit. Understanding relationship from the spiritual realm, from this spiritual perspective, helps us with our sonship position, authority, and all the elements of relating "one on one" to the Father.

In a later chapter, I would like you to try to do the business of relating creature to Creator by using "Father which is in heaven" and "holy is Your name" as an exercise. But for now we should understand that most Christians pray by supplication and a sort of adoration worship. Usually this is done using the acronym ACTS (adoration, confession, thanksgiving, supplication). The first part is very similar to the "Lord's Prayer," calling the practitioner to adore God. The difference here is that the focus of the above praying style is upon your own many words or meditations. Precious to any Father are the words of the Son, and with God's only Son Jesus, there should be little difference—especially when we bring them to the Father out of our individual hearts with our personality, which stays intact, although we are praying by way of a model.

His personal words of prayer are sacrificial because they are timeless and perfect offerings of Himself to the Father, so while you may offer your own words of sentiment to the Father, we are learning to offer up Jesus' words which are alive and powerful. There has not been a great deal of teaching on the opportunity to express Jesus Christ's prayer to God in this way. The methods of the past two or three centuries have tended to reign over the church, and it is probable that the former prayers of saints held intact Jesus' words.

Prayer is something we learn to do. We are not born knowing how to pray. We are not even born again knowing how to pray. We, like the disciples, must learn to pray.[25]

What an encouragement to the church today are the hours of sustained supplication by our saints, year after year. Their consistent, faithful prayers tend toward knowing God in a deeper way. This deeper mental conversation with God, praying for one another in prayer meetings, for the church, for the world, hour after hour, has had the effect of leading these people into deep-meaningful-abiding oneness.

It is here that the prayer warrior finds great warmth, the sense of well-being, and the glories of close proximity with the Father. These praying people have a joyful understanding that nothing else will quite satisfy them. Is it any wonder that supplication is a way of life for these people? Conscious or unconscious of these dynamics, prayer warriors pray for others, and things happen.

Often the hand of God is moved to action upon these petitions, though it may be admitted that their concern may have been God's concern right along and that it was God's purpose to interact regardless of the prayer. Yes, we are told to pray for one another, and change does happen. These men and women are thrust into the throne room, the very presence of God Himself, and transformation takes place. Surely it is the divine company we keep that sets Christians apart from the world. Proximity to God makes a difference and our prayers help us. In the August 28 entry of *My Utmost for His Highest*, Oswald Chambers suggests this:

> *It is not so true that 'prayer changes things' as that prayer changes me and I change things. God has so constituted things that prayer on the basis of Redemption alters the way in which a man looks at things. Prayer is not a question of altering things externally, but of working wonders in a man's disposition.*[26] [emphasis in original]

When comparing a session of private prayer, and praising God with a session of supplication praying, the difference with the intercessory prayer warrior is that this person has come to know God in deeper intimacy and often under the umbrella of petitioning for others. God calls us to come privately, with the purpose of loving Him solely in the Spirit. He wants us to actively choose to be alone with Him, in this intimate way, by actually choosing the times to come. We should say: I am "coming in" to this deep abiding relationship through the *Holy*

Christ, "coming in" by the door of the sheep gate: "he...will go in and out and find pasture" (John 10:9).

Every morning and evening this is God's calling, from Moses' tabernacle to Solomon's Temple, to know, praise, and worship "Our Father." Congregations of faithful Christians come in and pray in supplication for others before or in a scheduled worship service, and that is a good thing, but we humans were created to know God first, intimately, and out of the first and greatest commandment to love God first, with our all.

> *God wisely orders small events; and those that seem altogether contingent serve his own glory and the good of his people. Many a great affair is brought about by a little turn, which seemed fortuitous to us, but was directed by Providence with design.*[27]

Unlike the individual who has tried to know God intimately and has failed, the person who comes to know God by understanding what he's doing, how he has chosen to set aside sacrificial time to be *one with God*, it is he who is able to interact differently, creature to Creator. There is this sweeping anticipation of purpose, the constancy of relationship as it happens every morning. Christians can become joyous in the understanding that in a few moments of struggles, mind games formed as snares by the enemy, they will break down the barriers to private prayer. Moving upward, soon they are at the castle gate, through the doors, out of breath, and into the palace standing before the King, "Our Father."

Any sense of worthlessness is gone, replaced by the nobility of uniqueness that only knowing God's love in Christ can produce. Yet this uniqueness is not empty. One cannot stand in a special relationship with the Father without knowing others are there also. It is a great relief to know that we are each uniquely ministered to in this abiding oneness.

As we glorify the Father's name and understand our access to Him, we receive power as we understand our relationship with Him! God's view of us can be partially understood by studying the parent-child relationship. Knowing about our own relationships, father and son, can illuminate how God chooses to spend time with us. As children, we see this great big fathers presence, and the reality of his proximity to us can blow us away, thus, we learn our place is with our father. He has made this grand adventure for us so that we would succeed in coming to His throne and standing before Him in all His grace. Some of us recognize who He is and who we are in relationship to Him. Because of sonship, we have power to bring others into a right relationship with the Father! We are empowered to love as He loves. We are called to draw out the lost to Him because it is His plan as well as His desire.

The men and women who gain access to Him become trusted servants, those to whom He can give the very mysteries of His spiritual realm. As these mysteries unfold here, upon this earth, we become more sanctified. We become for Him those who glorify and praise Him and even win others to Him as witnesses of His Son, Jesus Christ. The Word tells us clearly, "The eyes of the Lord run to and fro throughout the whole earth, to show Himself strong on behalf of those whose heart is loyal to Him" (2 Chronicles 16:9).

He loves us, and we have come to understand that. He recognizes that as we see His desire to save the lost, we become lovers of what He loves. He brings people and circumstances into our lives, with gifts, to strengthen us by the power of His Holy Spirit *because* of our right relationship with Him.

He is happy with the idea that we love as He loves. He is pleased by the fact that we are righteous men and women through Christ. The idea that love is taking a dominant role in our lives is evidence of our love for His Son, which gives Him great joy. We come almost hand in hand with the Son to the Father in praise and worship, knowing who He is. He sees this loving relationship with His Son, whom He loves, because we are obedient to His Son and committed to sanctification as we are more acquainted with His Son's words, with Christ's presence, and leading. We set aside mornings for the "first things."

He watches us come before His throne and attempt to stand before Him and give Him praise and adoration, and He encourages us at each stage. He helps us become stronger by encouraging us to gradually exercise our understanding of how we are to know Him. He sends His Spirit in greater power, that we may know Him in a deeper way in our early learning times. He strengthens us, exactly as any father gives a child more authority, a deeper relationship, and more responsibility. Yet we learn, as we become more knowledgeable, He may withdraw His strength, causing us to become hungrier and motivated by hunger for the food of His presence, once so easily had, because of the consistent power of His right hand. So, we become changed, even spurred on by the great cloud of witnesses; we sense what is at stake for the one without hope, lost to the evil one. Such thoughts help us become stronger and crave to know Him more. As participants in the family business, so to speak, taking on more responsibility to love what He loves and growing as children grow, we become stronger, able to inherit the trust.

As my Father is in heaven, He lives in a place that I will be in. He is where I am going to be. The child always wants to be with the Father, and the Father knows that. Any loving father would make that possible; obviously, our God, our heavenly Father, did arrange for His Son to be the sacrifice for our sin, so that *all* who accept Him would be His children, would be with Him for eternity.

Wanting to be with the Father does not have to wait until eternity begins in heaven; you can be with the Father today. "Our Father" is about abiding in the blood sacrifice that continues to make your presence before God acceptable. As you offer up His purifying work, it is from the altar that His words, "hallowed be Thy name," cause the Father's heart to swell with joy. You are the bold ones who understand that you may approach the King as long as it is in the blood, hopefully with His Word, the sweet smelling aroma brought from deep within your heart.

The Son's words are what the Father loves to hear, and what we should stream in praise, not a string of mental thoughts bandied in acronyms.

13

THE WATCH

While practicing the habit of privately praying upward to God in intimate worship and adoration, standing is by far the best posture for keeping up abiding oneness. Above all else, because the Bible tells us to stand, we should be curious enough to bring our understanding of the procedure in line with this powerful truth. The humanistic viewpoint that standing is irrelevant should be regarded as without merit, for it has no solid biblical support. If you are in opposition to the question of "standing and praying," you shall have the opportunity to investigate the subtle leading of Old Testament and New Testament prophets, apostles, angels, saints, and Christ Himself as they lay witness to God's design.

Private praying in adoration of God while standing is the proper protocol before the Father and the Prince of peace, Jesus Christ! If you are not sure of this truth, I will say that you are not alone in your questions, strong concerns, or—for some—denial of the efficacy of standing and praying intimately the private prayer God longs for.

There are many who disagree, so it is right that we lay the proper historical foundation from a basis settled long ago in Jewish tradition. Most of us who read these materials are Gentiles, needing only to pause and reflect that we too have been grafted into the olive tree (the Jewish tradition and teaching). We too, therefore, are bound up in and by these truths to understand and receive our mercies, grace, and adherence to ancient statute and testimony.

It will be to our advantage to discover together as much as we can concerning the Word of God as it reveals a history of "standing." This controversial subject is wonder-filled and lightning-hot. It should be that way, for it is a sad reality that the twenty-first-century man has lost his sense of propriety, his plumb for proper prayer. The prayer of praise, worship, and the hallowing of God's name is a mysterious step into the throne room in heaven itself. This posture will support the *ablest* form of presentation of one's spiritual self at court. The Greek word for this sort of formality, as we have said, is *prosago*. This term speaks of the One who comes into court alongside His dependent, His friend, and presents the subject to the King.

Because it is unfamiliar, as we view this celebration, we come with our fear of acceptance and belonging. We are not the ones coming to court on a regular basis, so we are struck to our knees, bowing, kneeling, and groveling when we do come. We have little biblical basis to rely on concerning the proper approach to a distant God we may view as strict within a relational setting.

Consider a scene out of a movie depicting a young man courting a young lady in her home for the first time. The father looks down his nose at the youngster who is trying to be bright and proper, forgetting that in a short time he will be the son of the master. We are the sons and daughters of the King who delights at our appearance, whose desire is that we stand with the family, members of the family, one with the royal order.

> You did not receive the spirit of bondage again to fear, but you received the Spirit of adoption by whom we cry out, "Abba, Father" (Romans 8:15).

> Because you are sons, God has sent forth the Spirit of His Son into your hearts, crying out, "Abba, Father!" Therefore you are no longer a slave *but a son*, and if a son, then *an heir of God* through Christ (Galatians 4:6–7).

Standing is a must for the ones who understand the enemy's view, for it is Satan who has his methods of entering the mind with lies, often begun with good thoughts of the well-being of others, soon spoiling and carrying one off into the futility of the mind.

> Set your mind on things above, not on things on the earth. For you died, and your life is hidden with Christ in God (Colossians 3:2–3).

While attentive to God, a wandering mind soon yields to thought-life snares that neutralize the progress of bringing our sacrifice, our holy praise to the Father. Having made these points, we acknowledge that "praying privately" could be done in any other position under the sun. God will always accept your offering at whichever station you have reached, that place which you are best capable of bringing Him love. If you are more comfortable praising Him on your knees, go for it. Prayer, praise, and worship are spiritual; we are called to pray and worship in the Spirit.

You may *not* be able to stand, in that you may have a physical disability. Prayer, regardless of such a case, can without a doubt be just as vital. We know that other aspects of the natural body often fill in and take over with added help and support when limitations are present; here, we should expect the same outcome. The topic of the body's relationship as a *delivery system* of physical and spiritual substance is complex. We are into the realm of faith, which is the substance of things not seen; standing helps deliver it more completely. It may be illuminating for us to consider the standing position with attention to its feet, joints, and legs as a *platform* of the torso as though it were a living temple.

Let us go into a little more detail concerning ancient history—or, as a friend of mine likes to call it, the "old-time gospel"—as it relates to standing and praying. The material that I make reference to is easily found in the Word of God. The obvious nature of truth is that it is able to stand on its own merits. I bring this out only because truth can become hidden, layered in and among many other certainties and therefore difficult to observe and interpret. Some of these truths have been less obvious and awaiting rediscovery in their time and proper place.

I was delighted to find out early in this discipline that my Logos Bible software confirmed that the pathway I was upon was scriptural and correct. Not only was praying and standing *a* Bible tradition, but the descriptive evidences in the pages that follow are primary to the foundation of early prayer. The blessed prophets and the circumstances they encountered were the most glaring examples of revolutionary light in their time. After all, they were the ones who would stand when confronted with a Holy personage. I might add that these prophets and apostles were urged, even Spirited to their feet by a touch from these visitants. Consider the following Old Testament references:

> Bring me seventy . . . elders . . . Have them come to the Tent of Meeting that they may *stand* there with you. I will *come* down *and speak* with you there, and I will take of the Spirit that is on you and put the Spirit on them (Numbers 11:16–17, NIV).

> Then Elijah said, "As the Lord of hosts lives, Before whom I *stand*" (1 Kings 18:15a). And Elisha said, "As the Lord of hosts lives, before whom I *stand*" (2 Kings 3:14a).

> [The Levites' duty was] to *stand* every morning to thank and praise the Lord, and likewise at evening; and at every presentation of burnt offering to the Lord (1 Chronicles 23:30–31a).

> And he said to me, "Son of man, *stand* on your feet, and *I will speak* to you." Then the Spirit entered me whenHe spoke to me, and *set me on my feet*; and *I heard Him* who spoke to me (Ezekiel 2:1–2).

> Then the spirit entered into me, and set me upon my feet, and *spake with me*, and said unto me, Go, *shut thyself within thine house* (Ezekiel 3:24, KJV).

Notice, each individual in the above circumstances was *told* to stand! Having stood up, they would *then receive* their instruction. Standing, receiving; standing... receiving; standing ... receiving.

> Now as he was speaking with me, I was in a sleep with my face to the ground; but he touched me, and *stood me upright*. And he said, "Look, I am making known to you what shall happen in the latter time of the indignation; for at the appointed time the end shall be" (Daniel 8:18–19).

Wow! These kinds of encounters are no longer happening today, and we presume, have not happened since the close of Scripture at the end of the apostolic age. Let's look a little closer, with eyes wide open.

> Suddenly, a hand touched me ... And he said to me, "O Daniel, man greatly beloved, understand *the words that I speak* to you, and *stand upright* . . ." While he was speaking this word to me, *I stood trembling* (Daniel 10:10–11).

I would be trembling as well; how about you? Here are some references from the *Septuagint* (the ancient Greek version of the Hebrew Bible):

> And he said unto me, "*Stand up* upon the right side, and I shall expound" (2 Esdras 4:47a).

> So he answered and said unto me, "*Stand up* upon thy feet, and hear a mighty sounding" (2 Esdras 6:13a).

> And he said unto me, "*Stand up manfully*, and I will advise thee" (2 Esdras 10:33b).

This last reference is obviously for the crowd of jocks out there who like football, wrestling and MMA. This should give them something to talk about in the locker room! *Manfully standing!*

Further, the New Testament records these striking historical depictions in their obvious settings.

> Whenever you *stand praying*, if you have anything against anyone, forgive him, that your Father in heaven may also forgive you your trespasses (Mark 11:25).

Who among us has not thought about this verse in Bible study or when a pastor used the verse as an illustration or in some other way. Look at the context: it is intimate fellowship, the private fellowship of worship, praise, and prayer; A kind of princely "seal of confirmation."

There is a lot going on in this verse, and our focus is usually upon the forgiveness issue! If, however, our focus shifts onto the fact that Christ recognized standing as a valid method of prayer, the case for standing takes on a broader scope of possibility. Christ has just validated standing, based upon this text, as a part of the New Covenant and the New Testament church. Are you connecting with this?

> When you pray, you shall not be like the hypocrites. For they love to pray *standing* in the synagogues and on the corners of the streets (Matthew 6:5a).

Again, standing appears to be a secondary message gleaned from this passage! The absence of any negative reference to standing, apart from a desire to be seen by others, is all the more confirmation of this physical posture. Christ, in these two verses, speaks of standing as if it is an obvious learned, modeled, and practiced procedure that did not require a hint of exhortation.

> Rise and stand on your feet; for I have appeared to you for this purpose, to make you a minister and a witness both of the things which you have seen and of the things which I will yet reveal to you (Acts 26:16).

All the preceding references give us a wonderful look at these special people in their most astonishing and holiest moments. To be sure, they were very frightened of what they were seeing, of what they were hearing, and what they spiritually perceived. We can imagine their physical state, these men were hyperventilating, had racing heartbeats and chattering teeth.

Paul, it seems, would have his share of encounters. Jesus Christ had been in direct communication with him on one occasion. His first learning encounter was the miraculous confrontation with Jesus on the Damascus road. Accordingly, he was told to stand upon his feet and was then taken to "the house of Judas on Straight Street" (Acts 9:11, NIV), where he met with Ananias. There may have been others, but 2 Corinthians 12:1–6 best records an encounter with Jesus. Is it safe to say that Paul and these other men, over time, became a little more comfortable with each encounter and with the request to stand upon their feet?

Let us review the procedures of these encounters: There

is "the appearance," some supernatural being obviously from another realm enters the presence of one of these men. By comparison with today's lack of supernatural manifestations, all of us are unable to move beyond a basic comprehension of these circumstances and we are unable to shed light on the mechanics of such transportation, so we too become speechless.

The Holy Spirit in His wisdom has chosen not to speak out of the Word of God to explain how such encounters take place, so we shall only observe what the text is saying without further interpretation. These patriarchs, having seen these "visitants," then hit the ground trembling and are then *stood up*. We can all barely imagine how intensely an encounter with a supernatural being must have been to the nervous system, especially in broad daylight! Nevertheless, these patriarchs were deeply disturbed, uninterested in relationship with these beings, considering the apparent danger of such powerful forces. Life has a way of fleeting, fluttering, and then flying away when one is overwhelmed with this kind of superiority. The text tells us our fearful patriarchs were reluctantly ready to be commanded to rise and stand upon their feet.

Happy to be able to live another moment, they were now in the preferred position of standing. This seems to be the appropriate position our visitants want their subjects to assume, that they may best learn how to receive supernatural instruction. As you may guess, this has all the appearance of a protocol to receive revelation! Taken as a whole, the text has included posture as a key element in the process of receiving divine instruction. The physical posture common to prayer, praise, and the worship of divinity seems to be about a *platform*. Does this interpretation truly help us to understand the dynamics of praying?

To return to our major theme, we have reviewed these encounters and have observed what happens at their inception. Standing is clearly a part of what we are dealing with here. This is a platform for the reception of supernatural instruction. Prayer or communication with divinity has traditionally been thought of as an offering plate of our own design, handing it upward. Can it be assumed that these forms of prayer are actually two-way streets, if you will: *rivers* (plural) for our own useful needs as much as for the honored worship of God. Accordingly, it will serve us best if we try to stay focused only on a single aspect of these multifaceted gems of Scripture: divine encounters having their relationship to the posture of *standing*.

It is possible that the most important reason for this posture is yet to be revealed. Think of the rapture of the Church—gone! What about the souls that will be alone on this earth? There will be very many who are suffering! How will they cope? Where will their peace and comfort come from, if not from above? Will the standard practice of praying for these men and women involve more time upon their feet and less time in the face of evil? Is there a simpler, nobler, or more efficient way to gain the throne room and its respite?

There may be a part reserved for our dear Jewish brothers and sisters. After all, when we are raptured, some of them will have a whole lot of time to *stand* and look into the skies and wonder what happened to their raptured messianic brothers and sisters who left without them. It will be a difficult time, and our hearts should go out to these people, our chosen brothers and sisters.

In addition to these brothers and sisters, what about those who drift into the great apostasy of 2 Thessalonians 2:3, the great falling away? These lost children will only receive true and lasting comfort in reconciliation and communion with God—the communion of prayer, the prayer of adoration as the entrance point of divine fellowship, the "watch and pray" as spoken of by Christ Jesus in the garden of Gethsemane.

As we have seen, standing within these divine encounters, these relationships, was not optional; it was required, even compelled. These are presidential learning events that these people took notice of and were trained in—prophet to apprentice, priest to priest. They passed on that which was sealed into their hearts, the correct physical method to pray. It was a required physical principle, an action learned and carried forward by the students from their patriarch teachers, who were taught by these divine visitants, messengers of future events: a subtle yet direct instruction for the *correct learning posture.*

I would like to briefly add a number of obvious reasons why *these prophets and apostles stood*: Yes, it is manly! We are warriors, moving out from our earthly camp (the natural world) and into the perilous *in-between ground* of evil spiritual opposition. How many of our heads are lifted up in prayer and into the heavens? Progress has always been difficult against this sort of opposition. These ancient foes have been in the spiritual realm right along, opposing our prayer efforts century after century, while this sort of struggle is new to us. So it was with the prophets and apostles. The opposition in their day, as well as ours, is very strong. Standing was and is a connection with our higher power, but we know it must proceed *through* the ranks of a desperate enemy with influence over our progress. These prophets and apostles were pioneers, and good people die trying to carve out good roads while pioneering.

Here are some other strong reasons:

- It is *honoring* to the Trinity. There are but two positions appropriate for being in the company of divinity: on your face or standing. Certainly He is Abba, and when you see with the eyes of your spiritual heart and really believe that you can see, you will be in reverence awaiting His touch!
- It allows for the *most direct* spiritual focus: Standing straight is a *strong flowing* River of Water of Life that will, *over time*, take out any opposition in its pathway. Consider the simile that suggests the torrent of a flood's relationship to the river's crooked banks:

Teach me your way, O Lord. Lead me in a straight path because of my oppressors (Psalm 27:11, NIV).

John replied in the words of Isaiah the prophet, "I am the voice of one calling in the desert, 'Make straight the way for the Lord'" (John 1:23, NIV).

These references may not seem to direct your attention to the primary point of the physical posture of praying, yet their symbolic truth in principle is unmistakable. Prayer and praise are not static pools to contemplate! Your praise, elevated by the Spirit, is a strong torrent of faith-filled Spiritual Water that the body was created to express by faith, whether in torrential stream or calm, gentle mist. Worshipping God through the blood of the resurrected Jesus Christ can be a fountain of tranquility in a time of stress and storm. Intense and prolonged meditation is hard work. Yet the body was built for such a task as standing to pray. It is done with the biggest muscles in the body. Major joints—knees, ankles, hips, shoulders, and the neck—stack well in this temple formation. They do not stiffen, tire, or constrict the muscles and blood vessels as other physical positions might, especially when one's spirit is in fullness. The *abiding oneness* principle, whether of prayer or praise, was designed into the body, anticipated by God to be a posture for a vigorous relationship with Him. Praising God, praying, and worship are distilled from the heart, soul, and mind into a vertical "riverbed" of sorts that is the junction between heaven and earth: natural over onto spiritual.

Rivers and *fountains*, as described in the fourth and seventh chapters of John's Gospel and elsewhere, may be spiritual references to transportation from one realm to another. Consider the Old Testament reference that is often ascribed to the "Rock of Horeb":

> On the last day, that great day of the feast, Jesus stood and cried out, saying, "If anyone thirsts, let him come to Me and drink. He who believes in Me, *as the Scripture has said*, out of his heart will flow rivers of living water" (John 7:37–38).

These strong rivers within the believer, continues our Lord, are most assuredly of the Holy Spirit. That was the explanation Christ gave to His disciples in the verse that followed.

References like these, the Rock of Horeb, from the Bible carry with them powerful possibilities of a God who, by anticipation, laid down these pathways at the same time as He formed the earth's foundation. One day these connections between a man in the natural realm and the likes of the "Rock of Horeb" (as they presume relationship) will be as clear to us as they were to Christ when He spoke them. Also, we see a spiritual link in these two verses:

> When the Helper comes, whom I shall send to you from the Father, the Spirit of truth who proceeds from the Father, He will testify of Me (John 15:26).

> He showed me a pure river of water of life, clear as crystal, proceeding from the throne of God and of the Lamb (Revelation 22:1).

This River may be a suggestion that its source is at the throne of God and of the Son. The Gospel writers reference Jesus' words, of "Thy kingdom come." They speak of a method of spiritual intimacy with humanity by and because of the finished work of a seated and glorified Christ. Seated, which reminds us that His work was finished upon the cross—though He stood in grace and mercy, a sort of soldier's salute of respect for his friend Stephen while witnessing his stoning. Revelation 22:1 gives us a picture of the possibility of "river source" and our pathway to intimacy. These words answer our quest, our search for true purpose and meaning in life. They are answered in the Father, the "Headwaters," and in the Son, Jesus Christ.

These scriptures cry out for investigation into planned intimacy! Christ has told us in John 7:38 that "out of [our hearts] will flow rivers," and John completes the cycle by relaying what he sees in heaven as the "river of water of Life." The connection is overwhelmingly suggestive and mysterious. Here is a *type* of pathway from within the bowels of man to heaven upon the Person of the Holy Spirit. The Word is clear that there is a column of divine intimacy. Here is the complete fellowship of our spiritual heart, soul, and mind with God the Father and the Son. He is the Shepherd who leads His lambs to pasture, in and out (John 10:9)! Further, when the spiritual realm is engaged in warfare, the apostle Paul reminds me to stand with Him.

> Take up the whole armor of God, that you may be able to withstand in the evil day, and having done all, to *stand*. Stand therefore... (Ephesians 6:13–14; cf. v. 11)

"Watch and pray!" (Matthew 26:41) The "watch" is a military term used for a physical vigilance to physical dangers. Clearly we have a responsibility to see a possible enemy attack upon our defenses. From the spiritual perspective, one needs spiritual eyes to see spiritual enemies as described below: "Our struggle is ... against the rulers,... authorities,... powers of this dark world and ... spiritual forces of evil ..." (Ephesians 6:12, NIV).

As you observe this text, what do you say? Is it your "watch," and do you intend to take it while kneeling down? There may be many who take the watch in this manner, but that has never been the benchmark. Guards *stand* watch; guards are trained to be alert and on their feet. They must know what is going on around their post for the sake of the young, the weak, and the dying.

The argument may develop around Christ's prayer in the garden of Gethsemane:

> Coming out, He went to the Mount of Olives, as He was accustomed, and His disciples also followed Him

>...He was withdrawn from them about a stone's throw, and He knelt down and prayed (Luke 22:39, 41).

During this time, Christ was up against the unfolding events of His own sacrifice, knowing the time was upon Him. He was also on His face and on His knees in prayer. He was about to take the sin of the world upon His shoulders and accordingly prayed three times, in sweat and blood, for the cup to pass. Luke reports that He was ministered to or assisted by an angel for strengthening. This kind of foreknowledge unto His physical death, this asking a question of the Father while bringing the rebellious flesh under submission to His own Spirit, hardly offers a fair comparison of appropriate prayer postures for us. Christ in His encouragement to us in Matthew 6:6, to pray to your Father secretly, is addressing consistent commitment and a daily relationship, not the last rites of this garden scene.

So the argument for standing has clarity. With the spiritual eyes of your heart, look around you! Many are fallen or are about to fall in this struggle for spiritual relationship, for spiritual power and intimacy with God. The fact is this: most of us do not know that the battle rages for communion with God on such a profound level. All of us at one time or another have had a deeper desire to spend more time in private prayer, and who is it that opposed us if not the evil, wicked, spiritual hosts? I would add that many of us have suffered from muscle and joint fatigue from our poor choice of prayer posture. Also, I must say, you would look much better *standing* in Paul's "armor" than *kneeling*! Will you be caught lying down at the Kingdom's gate on your watch?

The Lord said to Joshua: "Get up! Why do you lie thus on your face?" (Joshua 7:10)

Therefore take up the whole armor of God, that you may be able to withstand in the evil day, and having done all, to stand. Stand therefore... (Ephesians 6:13–14a)

Does this sound like the battle rages even now? Does this also have the sound of future preparation for the coming of the evil day, the apostasy? Paul has called this day the day of evil! He goes on (v. 18) to encourage us to pray in the Spirit on all occasions.

Also, recall Isaiah's reference, "They shall mount up with wings like eagles" (40:31). An eagle is one moment perched, poised, and the next moment away, soaring, mounting into the sky. When was the last time that you sprang into spiritual flight from your knees?

These are some impressions I have of why these people were standing. So you see that our spiritual patriarchs stood in the presence of God the Father, God the Son, and God the Holy Spirit. They also stood in the presence of angels. I am sure that with a little thought, there are many more reasons for standing than those I've listed here.

Just as important as the physical posture of these individuals, whom we have referenced from the Bible, is the method of communication that took place. Consider that we are talking about spiritual visitants who have the capacity to communicate with us, whether they do so audibly (using a form of sound vibration) or whether they "speak," if you will, within the mind or heart. The form of manifestation is not important; my point is that the *exchange was done while standing*. Since these are spiritual beings, we can surmise that their communication is spiritual in nature. It must follow that in order to perceive spiritual things; one must be "in the spirit." Hence, we have such scriptural references as "God is *Spirit*, and those who worship Him must worship in *spirit* and truth" (John 4:24).

As you become strengthened in your spiritual practice, it will become clear that there is more than a coincidental relationship between standing and receiving, between receptivity and reception. Please notice the second reference to *spirit* in the above passage had a small *s*. Your spiritual person, the soul washed by the blood, must be the one interacting with God's Son and Spirit of Holiness, the Holy Spirit, or large *S*.

I have come to understand, from my own personal experiences, that being in the s/Spirit is an affair more of the heart than of the mind. Yet together, this union of purpose within the Holy Spirit functions perfectly while standing. There is a bit more to say about such elements and relationships, but for now let us move on.

Generally, the Holy Spirit chooses to come upon a Christian in His own perfect time. It is said, "the Holy Spirit fell upon Him." Often times like these are based on your own desperate need, personal praising, corporate worship, or some other occasion of Godly spiritual focus. Sometimes we are seated, at other times we are standing. My point is that at those times, it is up to the Spirit to choose where, when, and how you will receive His power, and when He will fall upon us.

God always desires relationship with us. Oneness in the Holy Spirit is no different! We should be the ones choosing when "we" are willing to come "in the Spirit" that Jesus might speak out of oneness. It is and always has been clear that He is there waiting for us. Nor is it a matter of our bidding Him "do this or that." He is pleased to minister to our needs, and we should wait upon His hand in graceful thanksgiving. He has not changed, nor will He! Revelation 22 proclaims this great invitation by Christ and the Holy Spirit, recorded for us by John:

> The Spirit and the bride say, "Come!" and let him who hears say, "Come!" Whoever is *thirsty*, let him come; and whoever wishes, let him take the free gift of the water of life (Revelation 22:17, NIV).

If we are to learn from these principles and grow closer to God, we must enter into the s/Spirit at the times of our choosing. That is not to say we are unwilling to receive the Spirit's gracious and timely falling on us in a fuller anointing whenever He chooses.

Will you come to the understanding that these principles are possible? Will you see them as probable, and will you *test* them? We have free will, and that's the way He created us. We need to come in and out and find pasture: "I am the door. If anyone enters by Me, he will be saved, and will go *in and out* and find pasture" (John 10:9). It pleases Him when we sacrificially come "in" to praise Him, to hallow His name.

The apostles and the saints down through history entered into the s/Spirit. As we focus upon the Scriptures, it becomes clear. The early patriarchs and prophets encountered beings of another realm, and they were spiritually awakened. These visitants moved among them with instruction, which formed the foundation of deep Spiritual communion.

Jewish patriarchs experienced deep spiritual communication,

and when an episode ended, when one of these encounters concluded, the prophets were left as before (returned to normal). But not quite as before; talk about an empty feeling! Again, in almost every instance, these communications were taking place while these men were standing.

In addition, it is my understanding that the filling or encounter was temporary because the Holy Spirit had not yet been given to dwell within human hearts for lengthy periods of time, at least at this point in God's covenant. By contrast, Jesus talked about and prayed for a more permanent filling in John's Gospel account, the 14th and 17th chapters.

We have observed that the ministry of the Holy Spirit seems to have been temporary, not a lasting relationship with these Old Testament figures.

> Do not cast me away from Your presence, and do not take Your Holy Spirit from me (Psalm 51:11).

David understands the comings and goings of the Holy Spirit. It does appear that the Holy Spirit came circumstantially, as it pleased the Trinity on any occasion. The prophets may have been, at some point, emptied of the Spirit, or His power may have been diminished. Consider Samson's powerful anointing of the Holy Spirit, enabling him to tear apart a lion:

> The Spirit of the Lord came mightily upon him, and he tore the lion apart as one would have torn apart a young goat, though he had nothing in his hand. But he did not tell his father or his mother what he had done (Judges 14:6).

The Spirit clearly comes and goes in His own power, time, and place. Accordingly, if these prophets did experience a diminishing of spiritual oneness, of this abiding power, I am sure they attempted to duplicate the circumstances by which they first encountered their visitors.

The prophets, and subsequently their students, must have tried to get into the spiritual mode, standing and reaching for the heavens, exploring for divine guidance from on high. I'm sure their attempts at reconnection went on and on. The patriarchs, and most likely their *apprentices*, became better able to focus their spiritual efforts.

All that aside, did the Spirit manifest Himself again to these early subjects of divine intervention, these prophets who called upon the ancient messengers to appear? We are not told this. What we do know is that the impact of spiritual encounters with standing prophets was so profound that standing and praying continues to this day. Look at our Jewish brothers who pray standing at the Western Wall, formerly the so-called "Wailing Wall of the Herodian Temple." Also, note the words of our Lord: "the hypocrites . . . love to pray standing in the synagogues and on the street corners to be seen by men" (Matthew 6:5, NIV).

There are many lessons to be learned from this passage, yet we shall focus on only two. The first lesson is obvious; if you are praying to be seen by others, then you have your reward. The other lesson to be learned is that *standing* was done in Christ's day. Standing, it must be assumed, was a practice seen in many places: in the streets and in the temple. We can also safely assume that praying upon one's feet was done in the home. Consider Christ's words in Matthew 6:6: "But you, when you pray, go into your room, and when you have shut your door, pray to your Father . . ."

If one stood outside to pray, then it follows that standing inside would also be expected. The work, the sacrifice of praying, whether praise or worship to the Father and the Son, is just that: work. Work of any sort has attached to it both physical and spiritual method as well as attending sounds. The sounds of private prayer are personal and may be part of the reason we are told to "go into your closet."

Christ reminds us in Mark 11:25, "Whenever you *stand* praying, if you have anything against anyone, forgive him." Again, we find two lessons to be learned. First, forgive! The other lesson Christ alludes to is the accepted custom of standing and praying. If there were to be any negative implication of standing, surely Christ would have given the admonition in such a context.

Matthew Henry writes in his commentary on Mark 11:25,

Note, Standing is no improper posture for prayer; it was generally used among the Jews; hence they called their prayers, their standings; when they would say how the world was kept up by prayer, they expressed it thus, Stationibus stat mundus—The world is held up by standings. But the primitive Christians generally used the more humble and reverent gesture of kneeling, especially on fast days, though not on the Lord's day.[28] [emphasis in original]

We see this custom of prayer as a procedure, passed down from generation to generation. Christ recognized this procedure during His lifetime. His recognition and verbal assent, it can be argued, are supporting evidence of this preferred posture. Is it surprising to see the Jews of our time who, while practicing Judaism, stand and pray at the Wailing Wall? Their rocking back and forth is a symbol of their connection with those generations long past, a sort of seal of authenticity. This practice has become the remnant of a great bridge, now crumbled; it is incomplete without Christ and the Holy Spirit and serves no other purpose than to be used as a springboard, launching generation after generation into the abyss of hell's eternal flame.

Once upon a time, such men climbed to the heights of heaven with great effort of perseverance and tenacity. Their energetic effort to beat back the spiritual opposition and to climb Jacob's ladder at all costs was rewarded by Spirit-aided flight. Those ancient messianic Jews understood Isaiah's eagle, soaring in praise and worship. The hours spent in focus and relationship with God in the Spirit through Christ became for them an effortless wisp of spiritual incense, their souls destined for oneness in His care. Their heartbeat and breath moved them ever so slightly as they perched atop the focal point of perfection in balance as they stood and praised God. Is this rocking back and forth that today we call "shucking 'n davening" a *type* of Jacob's ladder illustrated in swaying footsteps to heaven? This behavior, *standing and praying*, is an ancient time capsule crying out to be delivered to the generation which will take the time to understand the practical applications of this posture.

Many will say, "It is of little value what posture is adopted in the prayer of praise; what really counts is the heart!" I can see you reading these words and nodding in agreement. To this oversimplified answer I will also agree, in part. The heart *is* at the center of any worship, praise, or prayer. You are able to know Him deeply without standing. How deep is that depth of intimacy? The question still cries out for an answer: Why were the prophets told to stand and receive divine revelation in this manner?

We may say "Father" with our hearts, yet our soul cries out for intimate s/Spirit relationship, and we want to be told that we are loved. The teacher's lessons are best received in a standing posture. Read the word which cries out from your Bible; it is inescapable. We are told to stand and receive His Word. The wonder of it is that when we praise, we are also *fed* from His courts. You need to test this spirit. Your answer will astound you as Christ brings you closer to the reality of Our Father, within the closet, within the quiet room—upon your feet.

A. W. Tozer comments:

Within the human body were placed mechanisms for the purpose of communication with God Himself!

To look deep within these regions, is to strip away conventional investigative tools. The eyes of the heart that search here must be patient and sensitive and a bit first century. God has created layers of possible intimacy within us. Created beings, once they are sealed with the person of Christ, the name of God, and the power of the Holy Spirit, are poised to wrestle into that power. We are encouraged to come in, called to go through this narrow gate.

It will require a determined heart and more than a little courage to wrench us loose from the grip of our times and return to biblical ways. But it can be done. Every now and then in the past Christians have had to do it. History has recorded several large-scale returns led by such men as St. Francis, Martin Luther, and George Fox. Unfortunately there seems to be no Luther or Fox on the horizon at present. Whether or not another such return may be expected before the coming of Christ is a question upon which Christians are not fully agreed...[29]

If the Holy Spirit runs through human hearts like rivers of living water, then riverbanks like our living temple hallway to God must be understood in "The Tabernacle" sense, and then realized in private prayer. We must be reminded that Christ's words speak in an unseen and yet a knowable realm. Now that you have been awakened in these truths, and you are looking with your spiritual eyes, will you enter in oneness with Christ within.

Our loving God has offered up but *one road* into the Kingdom! His name is Christ Jesus. He is found in your heart as well as at the right hand of the Father. Jesus Christ's death, His blood, and His covering payment for our sins have met the impossible task of access. Our prayers now declare us righteous and able to join with the Holy Spirit in closing the gap between earth and heaven.

The noble and liberating high road of praise is the simplest and most rewarding of all paths. Simple, because God has enabled us to draw near to Him with the simplicity of a child. Rewarding, because it is God in Christ who awaits your praise, whose presence alone is the shower of His glorification. Stand, take your watch, and pray the prayer of praise. This will propel you into this spirit world and the fulfillment of Luke:

"At that time they will see the Son of Man coming in a cloud with power and great glory. When these things begin to take place, stand up and lift up your heads, because your redemption is drawing near" (Luke 21:27–28).

Begin this test; stand up and praise Him with your prayer. As the above word suggests, it is your time to become strong: He *is* drawing near.

14

APPLICATION

The usefulness of biblical truth, God's revealed mystery, must be translated, tested, and taken to the community of believers in Christ! The result of this sort of application upon people's spiritual lives is that it changes them! The temples of the natural world recoil in anticipation of God's inevitable cleansing power.

This chapter moves us into the notion that it is all about proximity to God. Even faith-filled hearts require time to look into the name of God, and this is why we stand. Proximity to God begins from within our hearts, Christ's home. His right hand holds the Holy Spiritual transportation to heaven, the Spirit of Holiness! Such power is a help for you, God's radiant power is an over comer of any hindrance of the enemy. The battle plans are issued, and yours await requisition. Please "stand;" you are next in line!

All of the Bible speaks, both Old and New Testaments, in the whole of its context, of the life of a Man who is also God. This contextual speech affirms many things concerning Jesus

Christ: His coming into the world, coming into His Mother Mary, and coming into those who were the first to invite Him into their own hearts, His disciples. These are a few of the wonders of this man, this God, Jesus, found by reliable sources of testimony throughout the entire Bible. He has come into many things, and chief among them is into our hearts. There is only one thing better than His coming in our hearts, and that, dear friend, is He will never leaving us!

"Lo, I am with you always, even to the end of the age" (Matthew 28:20).

Idou ("lo") is an interjection frequently used in the New Testament to call attention to something of special importance. *Egō eimi* ("I am") is an emphatic form that might be rendered, "I Myself am," calling special attention to the fact of Christ's own presence. Jesus was saying, in effect, "Now pay special attention to what I am about to say, because it is the most important of all. I Myself, your divine, resurrected, living, eternal Lord, am with you always, even to the end of the age."[30]

"I in you and you in Me" are phrases built of simple monosyllables, which, while simple, also drive the mind over into the complex world of the unseen. Our goal is to understand not only what these words convey to the intellectual community, but what they impart to a smaller segment of the Christian community. We should engage our prophetic community— the prophets—whose inspirations transcend the intellectual understanding of popular interpretations. "I in you and you in Me" is radical theology. God is leading us, inspiring us with these textual complexities that bring us closer in proximity to

Himself. Remember, He rewards those who come near with His presence.

To know God by your proximity to Him is to become empowered beyond humanistic reason. Do not be fooled by Christians who are the passive lovers of Jesus. It is their destiny to become stronger while on earth in a process called sanctification, becoming more like Jesus. This power and knowledge, useful now, will also be useful to Christians in another age!

Understanding, knowledge, and wisdom are powerful tools, but they pale when compared to participating with Jesus in the process of acting upon the things of tomorrow. It would seem that the so-called prophetic community of our day is more concerned with knowing what will happen tomorrow while they should be concerned with listening to the One having made tomorrow, Who holds its possibilities in His hand.

The Christian life is always about proximity to God in Christ, through the Holy Spirit. All the foregoing pages are relevant only insofar as they help those who will listen, who look to God in private prayer. These should learn how to pray in the upper room way, the way into the interior life of Jesus, the one abiding within.

> He breathed on them, and said to them, "Receive the Holy Spirit. If you forgive the sins of any, they are forgiven them; if you retain the sins of any, they are retained" (John 20:22–23).

In an earlier chapter we briefly considered why there was an absence of malice displayed by the writings of the disciples toward Jesus' persecutors. Look at the record! These men should have hated deeply these antagonists of their beloved Jesus; instead, they loved deeply as did Jesus so love the world. Not just their obedience to Scripture was at work here, but a sort of instant love affair with the world took place in the upper room from John 20:22 to Acts chapter 2. Apparently, Christ's blood was mysteriously placed within His disciples by His breath and His words, "Receive the Holy Spirit!" This *Holy Spiritual* office, sealing and saving by the blood of Jesus, was the power to know the interior Life of Christ. This extremely spiritual work was for the application of the blood upon these living temples and His future ministrations with them.

Before Jesus came into them, these men feared and hated the Jewish establishment! Yet when Christ said to them, "If you retain the sins of any, they are retained" (vs. 23), they did not act upon this inner power of the administration of damnation. Why? Not because they grew in love and became more sanctified, but because of the great love feast in the upper room and at the temple with their *indwelling Savior* for fifty plus days until Pentecost.

These exclusive powers (John 20:23) of application of life and death were then taken up by the Holy Spirit. "His" Holy Spiritual authority is then injected into man and searches for the lost in this "second things" activity. This is why most of our commentators have difficulty with John 20 and Acts 2. That the disciples' love of Jesus was so deep and personal with Him in this private way, loving the world as God loves the world, truly shows their heart in their writings. They loved their enemies as Christ loved.

> I, even I, am He who blots out your transgressions for My own sake; And I will not remember your sins (Isaiah 43:25).

> Why does this Man speak blasphemies like this? Who can forgive sins but God alone? (Mark 2:7)

Mark points out in the above verse that, by the scribes' own words, they unwittingly affirm Christ's deity. It should be remembered that though they question Jesus' right to forgive sin, what we also learn is that these men are versed in the various writings of Moses and the prophets. Were the scribes recalling Isaiah 43:25, just quoted, or Daniel 9:9 or Micah 7:18, all of which speak of God as the only one declaring righteousness and forgiveness of sin?

Praying privately, with focus from the heart or "bowels," does not seem so radical when one comes to grips with the claims found in the words of Jesus Christ. Notice in the above verses, we are reminded, no one forgives sin but God, yet the disciples are told (John 20:23) that if "*they*" forgive the sin of another, that sin *is* forgiven. Since the scripture above tells us that only "*God*" forgives sin, we can reconcile this apparent contradiction because Jesus is "*in them*" and "*Jesus is God.*" Clearly, these men are able to discharge forgiveness for a short time as a substitute for the authority of the Holy Spirit. *They will choose* to whom they will minister, whether they understand the cleansing blood out of the *indwelling Christ* or not. Jesus said to the disciples, "Receive the Holy Spirit," and by this act the Spirit was within them, present in the "first things," for showing them God, not as in Pentecost, choosing out sinners to save, some 50 days later. Speaking out of the indwelling Christ Jesus, alive in them by the Holy Spirit, the disciples loved even Christ's murderers.

It should be remembered these events were apostolic manifestations of supernatural events in *these men's* lives and only at this time. *None other* will experience such things at any other future time during the church age. The apostles of Christ were unique in many ways!

This Spiritual work offered by Jesus in the upper room after His resurrection is not a "second things" principle found illustrated in the branches of the golden lamptand. It is a "first things" principle found in the brazen altar and laver, a *type* of priestly work.

Divided tongues of fire atop the couplet branches of this lampstand are *types* of the spiritual offices found in the "Holy place" (within believers). These represent the "second things" which were illustrated in the Holy place of the tabernacle and would not appear until Pentecost, long after the disciples' interior love banquet.

SECOND THINGS

> There appeared unto them cloven tongues like as of fire, and it sat upon each of them (Acts 2:3, KJV).

Private prayer, abiding oneness, is hard work, sometimes bewildering and seldom taught with the aid of the Bible. Jesus Christ's death on the cross split the veil in the temple from top to bottom, which tells us that it was something God did. The Spirit of Holiness, upon God's satisfaction of the payment of sin past, present, and future, allows you and me to come into His presence beyond this veil. We are holy, clean, and covered in Jesus' blood.

> "Do you not know that you are the temple of God and that the Spirit of God dwells in you?" (1 Corinthians 3:16)

You should begin to move over into this new understanding of revealed mystery—to know how to understand, plausibly, blood brought out of your heart and applied over you as a propitiation, a covering actuated by the Holy Spirit. We are this temple property moving toward intimacy and then outward in power to deal with life's eventualities.

Craftsmen, in the colors of blue, scarlet, and purple, constructed the tabernacle veil. The veil also had illustrations of cherubim upon it. Such a veil was designed with foreknowledge of the death of the body of Jesus at the hands of men.

> Therefore, brethren, having boldness to enter the Holiest by the blood of Jesus, by a new and living way which

He consecrated for us, through the veil, that is, His flesh
... let us draw near (Hebrews 10:19–20, 22a).

We have a sundered veil in our temple because Jesus' blood, from the altar of the heart, is applied upon the mercy seat, making possible sacrificial access. The heart, as if it were an *antitype* of the brazen altar in the Mosaic tabernacle, is the same heart of the man where his s/Spirit (you, the inner man) sprinkles the blood sacrifice. The entire process is done by faith and is offered up into the Holy of Holies through Christ's blood, a fragrant offering to God.

As you stand before God, hands raised (hands closely resemble wings of cherubim), God meets with you between the two cherubim in the Holy of Holies. This Holy of Holies is not an ark but a place just above the ark, which ark is identified as the head. If the ark is a box with physical items of memorial in it, your head is the spiritual equivalent of this box with spiritual contents. Place the lid—mercy seat—upon it, with the cherubim atop this box, and you have, in *antitype*, the illustration of one's head. Hold onto your seat, it could get steeper here!

Since my hands are attached by arms, shoulders, neck, and a head, like a hammered-out mercy seat of one piece with cherubim upon it, I have continuity as in "one piece of hammered out gold." Like the wings of these creatures, so are our raised hands: the cherubim are spiritual *types* wherein God told Moses, "I will meet with you between the two cherubim." Yes, it is that simple and that unmistakable. Even the scholarly Bible community will sit back and scratch their heads at the amazing God they serve.

Eventually, all of Christendom will begin to apply "all things" to the record, adding spiritual truth to that which is revealed. Revelation or reforming doctrine is not as if we become such intelligent, scholarly types, but God remains on watch for someone in whom to be strong. It is a function of proximity to God, the leading of the Spirit by His abiding oneness. "We" decide whether God will use us by our availability, not as if it was decided that one or the other should carry the mail. None of those having heard God's inspiration, from out of the Bible, think it enjoyable fighting through the enemy camps while getting plastered by friendly fire. You should always know where to find such prophets, "too far out in front of their own lines."

So let us look up and see that, as did Stephen, the heavenly Kingdom is come there between your hands, just before your face. Do you believe it could be so simple that a child could see it?—and so simple that the seasoned Christian war-horse stumbles on this ground, and the heavenly saints are echoing the Scripture: The Spirit and the bride say, "Come!" And let him who hears say, "Come!" And let him who thirsts come. Whoever desires, let him take the water of life freely (Revelation 22:17).

It seems that we have some work to do if we hope to build for ourselves that place to be alone with God and abide in oneness, making His name Holy. Clean out a closet, hang up a sheet in the corner where you might groan out of the joy of godly fellowship. A trance is something you might want to share with your spouse or maybe your children someday. You should wait until you are a little stronger in your discipline before your prophetic voice squeals its delight. You've merely to choose to carve out the time, get to bed earlier and wake up earlier, and respond with a yes answer to this command. Love God first thing in the morning, as Aaron lit the lamps.

What will amaze you is how hungry you will become to get alone with God—the regimen of trying by faith, practicing your standing, looking up into God's face, and using the disciple's prayer to hallow Him—to Holy Him. The Holy Spirit, in Christ, is going to grab on to your little faith and multiply your efforts of loving Him, and you will learn what it means to "be still and know that I am God."

The prophet is not an antiquated relic with no future. God's speech is a continuous help for the teacher as well, illuminating the text for amazing sessions of instruction; for these *types* of ministers these inspirations will be a sort of "lamp unto [thy] feet, and a light unto [thy] path" (see Psalm 119:105, KJV). Who else will stand up for the Word and point out the error in Bible interpretation or church structures? It is imperative that "one who says what he sees" understand that such speaking out is subject to refinement or exhortation from other prophets. With an open spirit to others and a steady discipline of Bible study as inspirational grounding, the church-age prophet is ideally suited to speak out of the heart.

Are you the ones who are always seeing the way things should be? Trying to exercise what you may now know as prophetic gifts? Are you often making your case for what you believe the Scripture may be saying to the church? Telling others to their dismay how and why things should be changed, and which things they are? Even pointing out that it's time to change them? You may be growing impatient, tired of knocking your head against an immovable object for the sake of relevant change. I would like you to know that the Holy Spirit gifts us precisely for the good of the body, and it's your time!

Behold [*idou*], I am coming quickly, and My reward *is* with Me, to give to everyone according to his work (Revelation 22:12).

The prophet is the one who by faith looks to the heavens in anticipation of the coming glory of God. We must stand in our faith with our gaze at the object of Christ's command: Love the Lord your God with all your heart, soul, and mind.

Faith is the least self-regarding of the virtues. It is by its very nature scarcely conscious of its own existence. Like the eye that sees everything in front of it and never sees itself, faith is occupied with the Object upon which it rests and pays no attention to itself at all[31] (A. W. Tozer).

It is not an illusion that you are sometimes rapt in ecstasy and then quickly returned to the usual follies of your heart. For these are evils which you suffer rather than commit; and so long as they displease you and you struggle against them, it is a matter of merit and not a loss[32] (Thomas à Kempis).

While you are looking for evidence of abiding oneness, asking yourself whether you are having success, your eye has turned inward upon self, and you are losing ground to the enemy.

Far better for you to redouble your efforts to hallow His name by faith and "Just do it!" Stepping out in faith, trying to refocus on the name of the Lord, is the mark of progress. The Holy Spirit will delay His falling upon you, aiding your progress that you might by faith grow up. You are right where God wants you to be. His plan is for you to be on the ragged ends of confidence in yourself and upon the sure ground of trusting in Him for the needed faith in stepping into that perilous in-between ground of the natural and the spiritual life. Don't ask yourself if you are having success praying; *just do the prayer!*

For the ones who persist, there is an understanding of a few sensations that are quite normal and should be expected as the markers of progress. As you become one with the blood of Jesus (actually within you), you should understand that the uniqueness of this truth may momentarily cause you to pause in your pursuit of private prayer with God. You may find yourself resting in the great joy of the reality of knowing Christ Jesus in this special way. He is in you, and you are in Him, and when that understanding becomes the truth of this physical phenomenon acted out in the spiritual realm, you should not be faulted for a delay in your prayer session. A fountain proceeds upward and in the direction manifest in its ultimate purpose, which is a process bearing sensation, the fruit of oneness. The Word tells us He is the water unto eternal life.

> Whoever drinks of the water that I shall give him will never thirst. But the water that I shall give him will become in him a fountain of water springing up into everlasting life (John 4:14).

> If anyone thirsts, let him come to Me and drink. He who believes in Me, as the Scripture has said, out of his heart [*koilia*] will flow rivers of living water (John 7:37–38).

Anticipate the sensation of a fountain springing upward. You should be able to focus your intention upon God's name just between the two cherubim, with the sense of flow from your belly to the Father. This practice requires faith for the purpose of hallowing God out of your heart. It's an upward sensation, of the thing you are doing; remember, you are doing something, and that something is streaming the sentiment of "hallowed be thy name"! Your offering is not just a sentence in this prayer but the substance out of the kingdom, which has come into you.

Jesus' blood is come into you, and your holiness is from this abiding within. Your biblical desire to love God is a sentiment that we express through Christ Jesus by utilizing this Lord's prayer, this sacrifice of praise. Our sentiment, like a river flowing upward from the brazen altar, through the veil, and into the Holy of Holies honors God. This should be expected and actually focused upon. These are very strange activities as they appear on the written page, yet there should be a connection as you focus your attention upon the first part of this prayer. You should expect to spend 80 percent of your time on hallowing His name and 20 percent on the remainder of the prayer.

While your hands are in the air, there may be times when they burn slightly, become heavy, or tend to sway in a rhythmic balancing of the body atop this standing formation. These are additional sensations that may come upon you in a few weeks, may take months, or as in my case, may not appear for quite some time. I was not sure what was going on in the first days and weeks of this phenomenon and dismissed it as a blood/gravity thing as the hands raised and lowered. That was not what was going on. It is clear to me that power from the Holy Spirit, as it is manifest in the body, is very subtle and defines specific functions when they are viewed to be actual processes originating in one realm and by faith propelled into another realm.

I am reminded of how skeptically people watched the great TV evangelist Oral Roberts. There was something going on which we all admitted but were unable to understand. That there is power in the hands must be realized as they transmit the glory of God into the lives of others. Also, the Holy Spirit is a Helper to protect, and I believe this is one of the functions of the hands as they shape in fortification a strong tower into the majesty of God's name. It is as if your immediate place of dwelling, where you stand, is a fortress with battlements and towers, as if hands and fingers mark out the parapet on the heights of the castle walls. Here you become encapsulated in the Name of the Lord, a sort of strong tower upward above your shoulders round about your head.

Lowering the hands to your sides may bring relief to your arms and shoulders; this will do little to take away the previously mentioned sensations. Proverbs 18:10 gives us a glimpse into the spiritual phenomenon at work in this supernatural display of God's strength in a spirit-filled believer living out of this condition:

> "The name of the Lord is a strong tower; the righteous run to it and are safe" (Proverbs 18:10).

Daniel encountered spiritual opposition, Daniel 10:12-14 reminding us that our prayers are heard, our prayers are also hampered above. Unlike Daniel who interacted with divinity, we do not expect such treatment, rather we can learn from such testimony. Also we are told:

"Those who wait upon the Lord...shall mount up with *wings* like eagles. They shall run and not be weary, they shall walk and not faint" (Isaiah 40:31).

The Holy Spirit is the subject of these two verses, for the text clearly has moved us over into the place where the power of God is at work. Though there are many of us who, by faith, sustain their spiritual focus and are empowered by God for a witness to the hurt and lost, there may not be many who understand the power available through private prayer and the hands—these *antitypes* of the menorah flame.

I do recognize that many of the readers of these esoteric Bible interpretations remain in a state of unbelief, but that has little to do with the factual nature of these realities. Also, it is helpful to remember that these observations have a solid scriptural basis and are able to stand the test of scrutiny by simply applying some basic Bible research tools. Concerning the ones unmoved by these phenomenon, you will remember that this material is written for the prophet and not the doubter who rides upon such waves of skepticism. Test everything, we are reminded in 1 Thessalonians 5, and that this is not a suggestion. If you are moved backward in unbelief and hard against the wall, it is you who must test the most. You are commanded to search out the Scripture to enforce its integrity and defend its truth. With gentleness I admonish you: Do your homework!

Stand up and reach into the heavens! Just do it. How long have you recognized that your heart wants to know Him in a deeper way? I charge you with your delinquency of the love of God! How can I do such a personal thing? It is only because I, too, am guilty of this charge. I do not love God with all my heart, with all my soul, and with all of my mind. My words leap backward at me, and I am moved not to recant my charge that you may be moved upward and into right fellowship for His praise. The truth is this: He is worthy to be praised, and it is to your benefit to praise the Father in the Son.

The wonder of this practice is proximity to God and Christ Jesus to guide your steps so that following Him is to see tomorrow, today. He knows what tomorrow brings; "I don't know about tomorrow, I just live from day to day!" as the country song has it. That is what the prophets of today should do. They see tomorrow in Christ today. If you look, you will see! If you see, then you will say! The church needs her prophets to speak what God is saying to the church! Will you listen to God, that what you say today remains for tomorrow? "The eyes of the Lord search to and fro, for someone to be strong in" (2 Chronicles 16:9, paraphrase). Look up, your redemption draws near!

15

PROPHECY AND PREACHING

Let the Lord ... set a man over the congregation, who may go out before them and go in before them, who may lead them out and bring them in, that the congregation of the Lord may not be like sheep which have no shepherd (Numbers 27:16–17).

Moses understood the value of getting alone with God. We too need to go out, get away from our busy lives and go in. Going in to be alone with God empowers us, strengthens us and enlivens our Bible study times. It's how we see and understand the importance of following God's lead. This is that which we might call inspiration, God's spirit speaking into our lives. Accordingly, for our part, it requires going in to listen. You might say, "is this the work and ministry of a church age prophet?"

Divine illumination of the Bible text is how teachers, preachers, textual experts and scholars of the Bible minister to the church body. Again, the idea that God's plan has two parts working together is illustrated here. There has always been divine "inspiration" available from out of the Holy Spirit to help lead the church. Without it, the points of need in the church go lacking. Prophets are anointed to speak out for change. They are the servants who listen to God for such speech. As the above text suggests, they "will go out," leaving the people's presence, and "go in" as representatives," seeking the Lord God in private prayer for His direction and fuller understanding of Scripture.

Is there ever a good time for the preachers, teachers, and administrators to hear and be counseled by the prophets and act upon their proclamation? It would not seem so if we listen to Luther's remarks. He famously complained about the prophets: "They have a queer way of talking, like people who, instead of proceeding in an orderly manner, ramble off from one thing to the next, so that you cannot make head or tail of them or see what they are getting at."

Through the prophets, God cares for His church, continuing to speak through them, out of His Word. On the other hand, despite good intentions, even aberrant views of the Bible do creep into our communities, and the ones gifted in exhortation, edification, and comfort (the prophet) can be the source of these problems. Ever watchful, the prophet must be aware that Bible teaching is always a good thing. But prophets must also watch for the proper place and time when the power of God's application may be manifest. It is the Word of God, the Bible, that changes people's lives. The Word is life, as Jesus proclaims in John 14:6 "I am the way, the truth, and the life." For the lost person living in the natural realm, the doorway to spiritual life lies locked, sealed within the hearts of evangelicals who serve God. Only one person has the key for these men and women, and His name is Jesus Christ. His work completed on Calvary, there remains only the power of the Holy Spirit to call and bring to birth the ones God chooses to cross over the bridge toward eternal life. Part of this miracle is that the Holy Spirit allows us to participate in His task of applying cleansing blood to the new life.

The atoning blood of Jesus Christ awaits application into the new heart of each lost soul by the mysterious work of the Holy Spirit. In what time and place are such great things done? Is it the preacher who looks into the heart of the sinful ones and knows when and where they will find salvation? No! Is it the teacher who knows what tomorrow brings? No! Can the textual expert read into the text and find what words the unregenerate, lost and tormented one longs to hear? I don't think so! Does the scholar sift through the pages of history in search of relevant data concerning successful evangelism of people groups to whom the words of life were given? None of these fine people know which ones, of all those lost men and women, will be called out, chosen for salvation, their names written in the book of life.

None of us know where such transformation will occur and by whom the words of life will be applied? These tasks, like cloven tongues of fire, are resting upon the resident Christ, indwelling each believers heart and waiting to unfold in our own powerful part in the great work: to seek out the lost. We expect by faith, and pray in supplication, that the Holy Spirit will use our hands as ministers, like the winged cherubim searching out the lost. We cannot trust in our own efforts to seek the lost and find the willing heart that desires to reconcile with God. This is the Holy Spirit's work to be sure, but it is ours to be shared.

How often do we stop and really look into the Word of God

in consideration of what the Bible is teaching the church today. God desires that our eyes be opened by His Spirit for the application of the Truth? Without Holy Spiritual application, in its time and place, such revelation does not change much and is almost useless for the most difficult tasks. Utilizing prophecy to *adjust* the way we administer God's word in the church or community can be exciting, challenging and constructive. Our willingness to change pathways can only work if we are certain it is God's voice calling out for change. While learning lesson of "love" from 1 Corinthians 13, we also learn that prophets are capable of understanding all mysteries, and all knowledge by their faith. Why, because God knows all and chooses to speak through prophets. Our confidence is in testing God's prophets. They, above all, must get alone with God in Christ and out of His Word the certainty and unity of His direction will be apparent.

It has become clear to me that change is a difficult process—and most difficult while in the hands of the untrained prophetic minister. Also the principle found in 1 Corinthians 11:19 applies: "there must also be factions among you, that those who are approved of God may be recognized." This truth, that there will be differences in the way nonessentials are applied in the church today, must be understood to be a good thing, provided that love is added to the mix.

In the first place, the prophetic community should understand that they are messengers of God whose message comes out of the pages of the Bible. Second, these messages will usually cause friction while accomplishing the intended outcome, though their purpose and ultimate effect should be conformity to Scripture, unity, and growth. In addition, third, prophets should know that someone is always going to be uncomfortable with change; the challenge for prophets is to get used to their role while helping brothers and sisters realize their obligation to test prophecy. Fourth and finally, arrogant piety has been at the center of many conflicts in our churches today, some archly insisting on their way regardless of Godly consensus.

This same self-serving spirit with which Satan may inflame the church can bring ruin to any fellowship, or ministry, serving the schemes of the Satanic interloper who comes to steal, kill, and destroy. He has already destroyed many in the church today and broken many fellowships, serving only to gratify this world's need for self-satisfaction. We read in Titus the description of such a person, "They profess to know God, but in works they deny Him, being abominable, disobedient, and disqualified for every good work."

We seldom talk out of our hearts, out of our hurts. The troubles we face are often of our own making. Once we have failed or been ill served by some perceived unfairness, we seldom have the wisdom or the experience to extricate ourselves from the stress of the outcome as it unfolds like locusts headed for the corn. Often we become entangled in mental warfare, blaming others and deflecting the guilt from ourselves. These exertions drain the heart and mind of all strength for worthy endeavors.

Can we blame the modern thinking mind? Is not this the place where our reason finds expression in this world? After all, we've come through the Age of Enlightenment and the Industrial Revolution and have survived the cults of the "New Age," to be safely deposited at the outer marker of the close of the church age. We are without a doubt better off for all the great work of renewal from Luther and Calvin, Owen and Franke, Edwards and Wesley, the great shapers of the Reformation, and the Puritan and Pietist movements of the Old and New Worlds. The mind was well engaged in these movements, yet by the time of the nineteenth and early twentieth century we had come to depend rather on the evangelists, men like Charles Finney, D. L. Moody, and Billy Sunday.

As Richard F. Lovelace describes in his book, *Dynamics of Spiritual Life*, "This loss of intellectual mastery proved to be a critical weakness, since the secular humanist world view which had been in the process of construction since the Enlightenment was receiving powerful reinforcement from contribution of Darwin, Marx and Freud."[33]

In addition to the intellectual loss of wise navigation through difficult waters, we were to suffer spiritually in our prayer lives. Hear Dr. Lovelace:

> *The dynamic of prayerful concern for God's kingdom which had characterized the early evangelicals was replaced by religious forms and legalistic moralism, camouflaging the laity's ultimate concern for the feathering of their own nests rather than for the enjoyment of God and the advancement of His glory.*

The heart seems to have taken a backseat to this a powerful tool, the mind, designed by God to transact the affairs of this world from within His creatures. However, it is God's desire that we have free will while using this mental apparatus, so a balance of access was added as a sort of accessory. God has access to our minds, and to balance this free will business, He has also allowed Satan this same access. Without going into the volumes of material written or about to be written upon these subjects, let us just state the obvious and move along: Our modern minds are at work in the thinking state of interacting with the world whenever we are awake. God and Satan are also joined to us by our thought life.

People seldom look within, nor are we taught to reflect upon the one within pulling, if you will, the mind's strings. That person I'm talking about is the one staring at these pages from within your body and outward by way of the physical eyes. I'm talking about the conscious you, the identifying self.

My point is that the thinking mind is an amazing creation, but its usefulness is best assigned to God's system described in the Bible. How does the thinking mind become a dynamic tool of God for its greatest usefulness in the natural world? Numbers 27:17 a life system Moses learned from God , going out—taking time for God—going in—listening and praising His name—"that the congregation of the Lord may not be like sheep which have no shepherd." God inspires leaders, and Moses was inspiring Joshua! By application, the indwelling Christ from out of the heart best oversees the modern thought process of the mind while abiding with God. Note: The Hebrew's consider the heart and mind to be one and at the center of the man—His heart.

Do we truly understand the times in which we live, the purposes set before us as priorities? We *are* upon the greatest stage in all of history, apart from the first advent and the brief succeeding apostolic age. But neither our understanding, our wisdom, our knowledge, nor our "fear of the Lord" will hasten us into the next revival.

I believe that we will be the generation that ushers in the "fullness of the Gentiles" (Romans 11:25). Such a calling will lead us onto a pathway of recognition and support of our non-messianic Jewish brothers and sisters who must see their great tribulation. Their hope is in a tribe of Gentiles who, to be candid, are spiritually weak in loving the Lord, though they know the Bible through and through. This ragtag formation of the faithful evangelicals are destined to lead them to know God in a deeper way. Will they be driven to seek their Messiah more intensely because we knew the prophetic teachings of the Bible, and acted for them, or will the chase of Israel's enemy Satan prove to be too strong for many?

Given the general sense of our relational contentment in Christ Jesus, is our community missing out on what it should crave more than anything else: more time with Him? Are we satisfied with our glimpses of God and the easy relationship we share with Him? Or are we restless for the love of God that has ignited the firestorms of great revival?

As we gaze back at the testimony of prophetic speech, whole mountain ridges of revealed truth both recall and proclaim revival. The depth and length of her hidden valleys seem to promise the next great mountain ridge, and our hearts tell us, "This must be the last peak, and Thy kingdom come!" Have our minds become satisfied with the older, archaic interpretation of some of the more difficult passages that may point to a deeper understanding of the text? Do we really need more spiritual applications of truth? After all, what was handed down was good enough for our teachers and preachers, our parents and grandparents.

I fear that the traditional understanding of the prophetic message has not been enough for the brothers and sisters lost to the New Age in its various forms and fellowships. They have adopted a sort of dependence on physical sensation to verify meaning in life. Arbitrary emotional pleasure drawn from the world's system of gratification is draining the church of some of the most promising spiritual seekers after truth.

Does this sound more like a valley of shadows, through which the people push on through a blinding fog laid down by the winds of humanism? If there is one more mountain peak to strive for, should we believe for a renewal of spiritual power over archaic interpretations, for the view to be made plain by renewed doctrine or church structure? Will such revelation culminate in the sustained "joy of the Lord" with strength that will avail to rescue the weak and errant seeker?

The "war for the souls" destined to be sealed by the Spirit is poised to end in glorious victory. Most of us have not understood that a battle was fought on this terrain and won more than two thousand years ago, and many of us find ways to question the gospel's claims and rights. There are those who understand the fight and define what a noble battle is like. We have been so focused on the marching orders of past centuries that our weapons, though basically sound and powerful, are outdated and do not include such mighty engines as the Holy Spirit instructed us to assemble for the final push. My friends, we're talking about prophecy!

As mentioned earlier, Joel 2 instructs the current elders of the community that prophetic utterance will be added to the fight. If our spiritual eyes were directed aright, they would see the withering fire raking our ranks to a degree that would no doubt spur the angels in heaven to the defense, were they allowed to come. The mighty angelic forces have no fight here until their time. There will be time enough for the mighty hand of the Lord to level judgment after the Second Coming and the advent of Jesus with the saints at Armageddon.

God has been good to us, as the record will show, for not only has He given us the commandments and the statutes for our strength and resolve, but most of all, God told Moses to remember the testimony. Remember Jewish history, the record of the people's many skirmishes with the help of the Spirit of God and the "mighty men" of the Old Testament. The testimony resounds in prophetic speech of comfort in the truth that God fights for His own.

God is good, God is powerful, and God always wins. What we see repeatedly is the hand of God reaching into circumstances to show Himself strong on our behalf. Not that He joins the battle at the beginning or at the middle where we become overly dependent upon His strength, but at the beginning of the end of the battle, where those who struggle increase in faith and the strong become stronger in Him. There is this giving and taking of ground, battle lines redrawn, breakouts and flare-ups of the conflict, and they shall all one day cease. The time will be at hand, and both sides will know they are in the final push before the church is taken out of the fight.

Are we outnumbered, outfought, and awaiting our rapture? Shall we cry louder and longer to be taken home, justifying these claims of a swift ending on some notion that Jesus would rather reunite with us, call us home, and leave another soul lost to die eternally? Should we listen to others who say the church age is pretty much over with? Or will we see one grand push from the center of the conflict by an insurgence of power from within our hearts by the Holy Spirit?

What is it that can bring the apostasy to its knees? Has not this multi-headed beast had its way with the fringes of our harvest fields far too long? What is the antidote for this great desertion from the person of Jesus Christ as His church moves along toward oneness with the Father? Our great religion, as outlined in the confessionals and the creeds, has enough godly men and women engaged who understand Bible prophecy and are trained in the doctrine to receive a word from on high and act upon divine guidance. What must God say to us that will make a difference apart from what has already been said in His Word, the Bible? What could be said that has not been said that can turn our dead hearts from the cold to new life or a recommitment to the Christ? What word do we still itch to hear, what awaits discovery that has not been said? Is there some grand revelation waiting for our next generation of leaders to act upon?

What shall we look for, and where do we start looking? Will there be something so new and revolutionary that there could be no mistaking the Author's voice in its trumpet blast? Will God speak to us in a way that will be new and unmistakable?

We know something of what God wants to say to us. Starting from the "first things," it is that nothing has changed in Jesus, the Son. His Word will continue to bring newness of hope in Spiritual power, found where two worlds, the spiritual and the natural world, intersect. Why did Solomon, the wisest man who ever lived, say, "Vanity of vanities, all is vanity" and "There is nothing new under the sun" (Ecclesiastes 1:2, 9)? We all should be grateful, relieved, and even excited that we Christians are *to continue in service and relationship with Christ* and that He holds the power of the Spirit of Holiness in His right hand. If Christ and the Holy Spirit are the same ingredient of this new movement and there is nothing new under the sun, what is it that we are to look for, what is it that has the tang of victory to rouse the hearts of people back into joyous song?

Is it more of the Bible in all its splendor, mystery, and freshness of insight that awaits the studious pilgrim? Is it more Bible study applied to the record of the life of Christ daily toward revelation?

The Holy Spirit is applied by Jesus to our lives that we would know the Father and His will that His purpose might be supernaturally realized in victorious living. The enemy's defeat and loss of ground is what the world will know when we have learned to walk with God, by His Son, in the Spirit of Holiness.

What is it, what is the stuff to bring alongside of the Word of God for the fresh fight? Is it to be more of the Word of God?—meaning the Word that is known to be the Word, nothing newly added but instead revisited as if only now applying exegesis to get out of the text what the text is saying in the present age. The textual experts, the Bible scholars, refer to the tool set for this investigation by the term hermeneutics, the study of how texts ought to be interpreted, particularly sacred texts such as the Bible. Specifically, *hermeneutics* is the study of the methodology of interpretation—and by extension, the principles of translation.

Is it to be more of the Bible, that its rereading might empower us toward such application of its ancient discoveries that the world will be amazed just slightly before it burns bright red in fury and turns on us in anger? Of course the answer is more of God's Word, that we would more clearly gaze into its vast storehouse of wonders and amazing secrets never ending. More Bible, more Jesus, and being made more alive by the Spirit of Holiness.

The Bible needs to be read into the heart as well as into the mind. We tend to bring our minds into focus on the text while our hearts have not been actively participating in the kind of abiding oneness that unveils the deeper mysteries of the whole record. Without time spent in intimacy with God, how is it that you will receive from the Father truth that is only entrusted to the ones who love the way Jesus loved? Jesus took the time to be alone to listen to God, and the result of such proximity was this: God's reward was always with Him.

Scripture should be understood from out of the life of Jesus Chris, and His unwavering commitment to get alone with God. All that He did was fueled from this relationship and we should bring forward this truth in the newness of prophetic application. The Holy Spirit gifts the ones He will trust to speak forth, whether they know such speech is for a future context or not. These are the affairs of a relational God and His timetable within the context of the times appointed for us to clarify and apply these truths.

To be sure, the original copies (autographs) of the Bible may never be ours to muddle through, grovel before, or pontificate as sacred apostolic merchandise. God, in all his wisdom, caused every one of the autographs to be worn out or lost to us—for our good. We are left with the Scriptures as they were copied and recopied, coming down to us as our collections of sixty-six books, the Bible.

The answer to all the above questions concerning God's speech to us at the close of the church age, the times of the fullness of the Gentiles, can be summed up in this one verse: "Eye has not seen, nor ear heard, nor have entered into the heart of man the things which God has prepared for those who love Him" (1 Corinthians 2:9). This speech is for the living, not only for the raptured church or the church of the seventieth week of Daniel. It awaits our spiritual eyes and ears!

Referring to "the things which God has prepared for those who love Him," the Scripture continues: "But God has revealed them to us through His Spirit. For the Spirit searches all things, yes, the deep things of God. For what man knows the things of a man except the spirit of the man which is in him? Even so no one knows the things of God except the Spirit of God" (1 Corinthians 2:10–11). "But God has..." and even if we stop here, we see that He has already revealed the things that the eye has not yet seen, that the ear has yet to hear.

What is it that we can expect? It is more of the Bible... Yes, it is more—or better yet, it is that which we have heard with our physical ears and seen with our eyes. In our day it is the same text, only now, in this time, it will be our spiritual eye that will see and our spiritual ear that will hear. God is saying, *Just hang on; I am at work over here, and these works you know of and you have heard of and they are revealed, yet I am still speaking these words.*

What we have read in the preceding paragraph is just what we are hearing in Paul's letter. What we are looking for is what we have heard in the pulpits for years. What we have heard is what Christ talked about in John 10: "My sheep hear My voice ...and will go in and out and find pasture" (verses 27a, 9b). You and I have heard His speech from passages of the Bible as our preachers, teachers, and mothers and fathers have taught us over and over again how we ought to live.

We are given a glimpse of the future of God's children, to whom is promised revelation! Listen to the following verse in this chain of spiritual events. "... we have received, not the spirit of the world, but the Spirit who is from God, that we might know the things that have been freely given to us by God" (1 Corinthians 2:12 NKJV). This verse is telling us that our help is truly from God and not of this world. Supernatural mysteries are all around the ones who believe and speak out as His witnesses. Just prior to Paul's helpful declaration, we read this: "But God has revealed them to us *through His Spirit*." This sort of reference to such revelation is confined to the supernatural realm. The Spirit is the one from whom these mysteries and spiritual gifts are carried, and we must stop there because there is much confusion over the interpretation of this Scripture. From a casual reading of the text as well as, in many cases, the partial understanding offered by a commentator, it appears as if the author of the Word or text is the Holy Spirit. The Holy Spirit is not interested in giving His opinion, advice, or knowledge over and beyond that which Jesus Christ has spoken.

We read in John 16:13 (KJV) that, as Christ discusses the coming Holy Spirit, He tells His disciples: "When he, the Spirit of truth, is come, he will guide you into all truth: for he shall not speak of himself." His discourse continues: "He will glorify Me, for He will take of what is Mine and declare it to you" (verse 14). And elsewhere: "He will testify of Me" (John 15:26).

It is and has been a mistake of the church and its understanding of such references to the Holy Spirit to ascribe authorship of God-breathed Scripture to the Holy Spirit. It is of Him (Jesus Christ) that the Holy Spirit speaks! It is of Christ Jesus from within each of us that the Holy Spirit awaits instruction for the application of His own blood upon the sinful heart and then upon the affairs of mankind. In other words, the Holy Spirit is not interested in drawing any attention toward Himself and away from the finished work of the Son of Man, Jesus Christ. We must learn to listen to Jesus and then the power and the know-how of the Holy Spirit will carry that voice. This communication is for us to use now and in every place where faith finds expression. It is in anticipation of reforming church structures and dead orthodoxy that we seek the voice of Jesus' words to be revealed in newness by the Holy Spirit.

Having stopped, shall we continue where we left off? Are we to understand from this passage that we have a sort of delivery system that does not fail? He is within us and can be upon or next to us. John 14:16–17 tells us, "He will give you another Helper ... the *Spirit of truth ... who ... dwells with you and will be in you.*" These are the complex relationships between two worlds, the spiritual world breaking supernaturally into the natural world. This is a place that our busy mind will overlook unless it is sensitized as we dwell on the Word and let our hearing produce faith. So then faith *comes* by hearing, and hearing by the word of God (Romans 10:17).

What would you give for the ability to see tomorrow on a regular basis? All that you did today would stand the test of time and bring no end to the successes of your decisions. You would give all you had because you would know that what you gave would come back to you a hundredfold. The problem with that scenario is that you would wreck the work of the building blocks that have become your tower of faith. This seems to be the stuff that we are here to build with. We are not to see tomorrow's events today, so that our *faith* will increase with spiritual sightedness.

Yet the facts are, first, that we *can know* what to do and, second, that what is done today *will* remain standing tomorrow. When we have understood enough to rely upon the Holy Spiritual giving of the truth and apply it to our tasks, God's lasting purposes are brought to pass as a result. Of the vast record, all of the sixty-six books of the Bible, Then again, *what* are the verses that I should be looking for, and of all of the possible places for such Scripture to be applied, how will I know *where* it is to be useful? This is certainly an imposing task, for such an important cause to be left to weaklings like ourselves. Yet that's where we find ourselves, because that's how the Father made it work.

Is it a good idea to look into the Old Testament for clues as to how to live for today? Of course the answer is yes! For one reason, things seem to have been less complicated back then. Another reason is that a thread running right through the Old Testament is the theme of loving God and of God loving his children. What a wonderful place to begin to look for answers to the complex issues of our time. Loving God and God loving his children made for great success stories.

What were some of the lessons His children learned back then, and what were the lessons the world learned? His children seemed to finally get the idea that it was always to be God first and something else second! For those who were not of the house of Israel, it was always: "If the children are loving God with their all, doing the 'first things,' don't mess with them. Their God is big and bad, and you won't prevail against Him. However, if His children are disobedient with Him, have your way with them. He doesn't seem to care that much during those times, and He may even help you push them around." The evidence suggests that loving God is a touchstone issue in the Old Testament, and today it might well be a good place to begin the pursuit of another reformation.

Earlier we talked about how useful the head is in this world and how useful the heart is to the supernatural spirit world. I understand that in the next few paragraphs we will be crossing a few eyes and raising as many eyebrows. However, if we are to uncover what is actually being said in Scripture, we run the risk of offending some and leaving them behind as naysayers. Such skeptics often cling to dead orthodoxy—such as is common in the church today.

The prophetic gifts of edification, exhortation, and comfort applied to the church-over time-with good application, change lives. Who are those steady, unwavering ones who are to apply the anecdotal balms of healing, the words of life and correction? "First apostles, second prophets, (and) third teachers" (1 Corinthians 12:28, NKJV), and of these, apostles are no more. We may find functionaries with pomp and entitlement, yet they are devoid of apostolic authority and power.

Here, Paul the apostle, writes to the church of the gifting of the Holy Spirit for application of the greatest good of the church body. We find the same construction in other lists in his epistles as if the first, second, and third gifted members are given in that order, not randomly, but for a reason. In the historical record of the activities of the church, Paul's admonition about the importance of prophecy for the church is available for study. For the past two thousand years we have not seen the prophetic membership active in the church—certainly not with the favor shown the other gifts in the first century or two.

Was the lack of prophetic influence a surprising outcome to God and His Son? The bishops and church fathers and the pastors and teachers of our day have all placed the prophetic messenger at the back of their glorious train, and God understood it would be so, now as then. All of us understand that the church did and will continue to encounter many problems with the "future proclaiming" false prophets. This may be one reason the prophetic community participates formally in practically none of the public aspects of evangelical church structure and ministry.

This situation may change, and the more so as we approach

the close of the church age. We have all read Peter's great sermon from Acts 2 where he informs us of the prophet Joel's words concerning the latter days. Some of our messianic Jewish brothers and sisters have prophetic gifts, as do many charismatic Catholic and Protestant believers around the world, and from the Bible they will bring to the community the revelation of God's word confirmed by Joel (2:28–29): "I will pour out My Spirit on all flesh." Joel tells us that the Jew and the Gentile will prophesy! Listen to his words: "Your sons and your daughters shall prophesy." Is Joel speaking to the Jewish sons and daughters of the descendants of Abraham, Isaac, and Jacob? Who are these "menservants" and "maidservants" of whom Joel speaks? Peter repeated these words (see Acts 2) to the representatives of all nations gathered in Jerusalem, from Mesopotamia to northwest Africa. Is Joel addressing as well the Gentiles of our day who await their participation in the transformation and reformation of our church and her doctrine? Such change begins out of the creedal statement of historic Judaism with the basics of our Christian faith. The *shema*:

> Hear, O Israel: the Lord our God is one Lord: and thou shalt love the Lord thy God with all thine heart, and with all thy soul, and with all thy might (Deuteronomy 6:4–5, KJV).

What could be simpler while at the same time so far from the lips and understanding of the leaders of our time? We hear of how much we love God and are willing to show Him our love, even testifying to the wonderful works done in His name. Admittedly, these are good things to do, especially when you realize most of this work is done in our own power. Yet where is the forty-five-minute sermon on the practical teaching of "How to Love God" intimately?

When was the last time we all sat together and listened to the pastor teach on prophecy as a reality found and practiced in the New Testament—not the Old Testament "future speaking" toward a future generation, but the prophecy of the New Testament that speaks back toward the Bible from the life of Christ and into the lives of His body, the church? Wouldn't we serve each other the more if the children of God learned to listen to the voice of Christ out of His Bible and desired to prophesy such truth?

To prophesy in this age, one must understand a few of the basics. It is best if you are gifted in this area, for Scripture tells us that not all are able candidates of prophecy. Moses said, "Oh, that all the Lord's people were prophets and that the Lord would put His Spirit upon them!" (Numbers 11:29), a sentiment shared by Paul (see 1 Corinthians 14:1, 5). Further, you need to have something to say! Unless you are to be a false prophet, you had better speak out of the Bible. The closer you stay to Scripture, the better.

Lastly, to be inspired by the Holy Spirit presupposes you are a child of God—born from above by the Holy Spirit, who washes you sinless with the blood of Jesus. I personally believe in the biblical evidence of linkage from the apostolic fathers with the laying on of hands for commissioning and empowering subsequent ministers and prophets of Christ. This would fall into the category of a nonessential belief while holding to a tradition of passing down in an unbroken succession the original fire of divided tongues upon today's saints.

It should be understood by most of us that our inspiration comes from the Father and is applied from an abiding relationship. When you look, you will see; when you see, you will say! It is a simple process in which prophets who understand their gift look back at the progress of their relationship in Christ, and by Holy Spiritual power, there occurs inspiration. Rather than lightning from a bottle, prophecy is cumulative in its methods of observation; one thing upon another until the thing is in possession. It may very well have been said: "God never simply gives us an answer, He puts us on a line where it is possible for Truth to break more and more as we go on." Should we be surprised that as we go on in observing truth out of the Bible, day by day the Holy Spirit speaks what Christ has placed upon a *type* of *table of showbread*, our daily bread, food for us and our neighbors that we might become one with the Father.

To assume the commission of prophecy on your own and from your own understanding of Scripture is difficult because of two things. The first is that the enemy will place obstructions before your mind hindering abiding with the Father in Christ and he will dissuade you, often with fiery darts, from this discipline. The second thing is that our community's teachers and preachers have little understanding of prophecy (most likely because it has not been taught to them) and are ill prepared to teach prophets. They know of the prophetic gift but are not gifted themselves, lack the time to invest in its understanding, and in any case find prophecy impractical for their methods of shepherding their flocks.

Paul reminds us that the spirit of a prophet is subject to that prophet—self-control and order have their place in a prophet's life and ministry (see 1 Corinthians 14:31–33). One reason is so that the church might be enabled to understand how to apply a prophetic message. It may also be appropriate for these people to teach each other out of their righteous experiences, since Holy Spiritual influence once understood is a by-product of exercise and training. While teaching may go either way, prophetic messages should be welcome, but preachers, teachers, and executives should mediate how they are applied to the body. What is interesting is that these preachers have little understanding of how such gifts should be used in the church today. It's a sort of circular problem in that the preachers need the prophets to prophesy from the Word of God, and the Holy Spirit wants to use the prophets, and the preachers need to learn how to listen.

> "Do not quench the [Holy] Spirit. Do not despise prophecies. Test all things; hold fast what is good" (1 Thessalonians 5:19–21).

Let's take a look at a few prophetic examples that have been around for a while in the church of our day. When the choir or the worship team or the musicians lead out in worship and praise on Sunday morning, what is heard is a form of contemporary prophecy. The words, it is hoped, are the product of biblical truth and divine inspiration toward righteous people. The tone, melody, and chorus are Holy Spirit–inspired. What about the "life lessons" acted out in short plays upon the stage next to the pulpit on Sunday morning? Is that a sort of prophetic message inspired by the gift of prophecy for the edification, encouragement, and comfort of the persons needing ministry of the Word of God portrayed by actors? Have you been filled with joy while watching film or a media presentation from a Christian resource that depicts the life or times of Jesus? Isn't that another form of prophecy? The *preachers* and *teachers* of our formal gatherings should look harder at expanding these powerful means of communication and spend less time lecturing, which has always been understood as one of the least effective ways to impart facts or information to a seated audience.

Is there a place for the prophet to speak out in public gatherings of all kinds, especially in the traditional church of our day? Paul seems to think so: "You can all prophesy one by one, that all may learn and all may be encouraged" (1 Corinthians 14:31).

Take for example the potential for the false prophet, speaking out in a gathering, who would lead the weak person away from the truth. What about the problematic accusations of misuse of time better spent on other more valuable learning experiences? Will the untrained prophet stutter and stammer, not qualified to speak out in these meetings, creating all sorts of new problems? What of the unprofessional appearance of the disheveled and out-of-place speaker, perhaps hurting attendance, drawing off much-needed revenue from the tithes of the wealthy who will not tolerate the charismatic look of these esoteric behaviors?

I belong to a conservative body of believers. We are not necessarily charismatic, although we do believe in the supernatural powers attached to our faith. Our pastor is practicing many prophetic applications of the Word of God in our Sunday worship services, and it is quite inspiring to watch God leading him. This young man is bringing to life the first century church here in Southern California in one prophetic step after the next.

Knowing that we have a responsibility to practice the whole teaching of the Bible, we are faced with a troublesome problem. What is the wisest way to reclaim this important gift, the prophetic message, from its limbo of scorn and neglect? After all, this is the Holy Spirit reaching out from the Spiritual realm right down and into the natural realm with the power of God to lift our hearts into the day.

Hopefully, we can call upon a responsible prophetic community to help us out with their clear spiritual sight of applying Scripture to the contemporary problems of our times. There will never be a lack of power applied from the kingdom of God to counter the weak and feeble assaults from the forces of Satan. God's healing hand, strong arm, and foreknowledge of the events occurring tomorrow will always win out, thanks to the few who have learned to listen today.

May I suggest that with a "tech" person informed and taught how prophecy can work within the church, the preachers and teachers could do wonders to shed light on such problems. Using the media department, one could preprogram interviews from the body, to gain and transmit the needed value to be drawn from the life experiences. Ask the leaders of your support groups and Bible study sessions to be aware that some people in these groups have prophetic gifts. These members should be considered as candidates to take part in public proclamation. They have access to "the testimonies" which Moses was instructed to remember.

It will take courage for those within the body who are going through difficult times to share intimate moments and situations that may be embarrassing or appear shameful. When those prophetic facilitators and interviewers are available and understand their roles, they should come alongside those who are hurting, those wanting to share their fears, burdens and success. The prophet purposes to help those sharing their message, that while they may be in the beginning stages of pain, and while others are in the middle, and still others at the end, all of us are inspired to pray, support and be encouraged by the experience;

In any event, the teaching value is without measure to the whole body if prophecy would be considered a viable sharing experience, whether live or taped for later broadcast. This is just one example of a wide variety of choices. Administrators and pastors should consider the counselor's role; the spiritual or psychological helper opportunities that are everywhere in the church today.

All of us should aid in the work of the prophets, looking for incidents that might provide teaching moments. In the larger churches, a regular gathering of mature and gifted prophets should rule on what works with (or corrects) the direction of the church, especially the pastor's message series, and the veracity and timeliness of each speech of prophecy for the church. Select the appropriate messages to be taped by those with prophetic gifts, and air them in the public meetings. Worship segments and coordinating songs with these visual prophetic moments will greatly increase their spiritual impact, as all together we learn what the Spirit is saying to the church. This is a way to begin using prophecy in such difficult and complex times as we face.

We understand that Satan would want these issues kept in the dark. Truth and wisdom confirm that these situations are valuable as teaching tools, opportunities for us to remind each other that "in the world you will have tribulation" and that it is a normal part of the spiritual life. Such opportunities answer to the latter part of the verse: "be of good cheer. I have overcome the world" (John 16:33). Those going through the circumstance gain hope as they see God using them to encourage and teach others. Others see their bold commitment to live righteously and obey Scripture.

Our times, as stated earlier, have been governed by a cold taskmaster: "the head" and its thinking mechanisms of the mind. Tending to the need of our conscience to be cleansed, washed by confession as it is soiled in the world, is a full-time job. Add to the contents of our minds the fiery darts the enemy hurls at us as reminders of our failures, and it doesn't take much for gloom, negative thoughts, and fears to keep us in mental bondage.

Control of this mental apparatus must be yielded to the truth in Scripture applied by the Holy Spirit's power as we abide in Christ in oneness. To be more like Christ, especially during the most difficult times of our day, is done out of the heart—Christ's home. "Practicing the presence of Christ," or "(to) be led by Christ" or a number of other thoughts upon this premise should be understood as: "the heart managing the mind" in the natural realm. In the community of Christ, we have been given a new heart which was prophesied long ago, and it is the will of the Father that the heart be in oneness with Christ, bringing into submission the human will. We live in the natural world where our mind guides our daily progress. The plan of God is for us to have a spiritual heart, translating to us and enabling us to put into practice the truth, the righteousness, the wisdom, and above all the love of God in our lives. The heart must lead out with the higher biblical values to make proper choices in the natural world. Christ should always be the source of the creativeness of the mind as we interact in the world, while the Holy Spirit orchestrates the choices creature to creature.

In sum, it is the Bible we come back to for clarity. Its text is unchanging yet in need of Spiritual inspiration by the prophetic community. Hopefully, they will interpret it, study it, and wait upon the Lord in abiding oneness, that by these gifts, they too may stand with the preachers, teachers, and administrators of the community who practice loving God and loving one's neighbor through biblical illumination.

16

THE NAME

Loving God intimately is unlike anything we understand, certainly unlike loving anyone we know and, by way of biblical example, far more spiritually subjective than we would ever have thought. Jesus, the *Holy* Christ, came into a physical body that He might help us. How is this to be, since we are commanded to love God spiritually and this while we are in the natural realm? It comes down to this: We've got to get over to the spiritual side of loving God, becoming sacrificially obedient to a Spiritual God.

Let's turn our observations to what Jesus Christ said to Philip, one of his hand-picked twelve: "Philip said to Him, 'Lord, show us the Father, and it is sufficient for us'" (John 14:8). John reminds us that we are not alone in our desire to know the Father; to have a relationship with the God of Abraham, Isaac, and Jacob.

> Jesus said to him, "Have I been with you so long, and yet you have not known Me, Philip? He who has seen

Me has seen the Father; so how can you say, 'Show us the Father'?" (John 14:9)

As noted in the earlier chapter, "The Tabernacle": "*We must stay close to the shoreline where we shall not be sunk down and lost in folly.*" Understanding the implications of "the Name" of God requires a voyage into the deepest parts of Scripture. The above verse tells us, "He who has seen Me has seen the Father," which may create more questions than our knowledge is able to comprehend let alone answer. Therefore, we venture into a place where the eye may see only dimly.

> Father, the hour has come. Glorify Your Son, that Your Son also may glorify You, as You have given Him authority over all flesh, that He should give eternal life to as many as You have given Him. And this is eternal life, that they may know You, the only true God, and Jesus Christ whom You have sent (John 17:1–3).

The power of God, which includes the name of God, reminds us that this name has authority over "all flesh."

> Now I am no longer in the world, but these are in the world, and I come to You. Holy Father, keep through Your name those whom You have given Me, that they may be one as We are (John 17:11).

Further, we see that the King James and New King James versions of the Bible place believers in the name of God, *kept* (watched over, protected, guarded, observed attentively). Christ is imploring God to place believers in a spiritual place of safety: Hold them in *the Name*, God's reputation, fame, and glory.

This state of keeping is one of sustaining. The apostles and other believers are placed in the Name while Jesus is away. Whether away preaching in the underworld or afterlife or away until He can come into them and abide (*meno*) we cannot say. *Keeping* is God's spiritual power facilitating abiding oneness, and that can be understood to be the *power* of protection, as translated in the NIV: "protect them by the power of your name—the name you gave me—so that they may be one as we are one" (John 17:11).

This is not protection from flesh and bones but protection from evil: "keep them from the evil one" (John 17:15). Power for abiding is in the Name, and we are helped by this supplication of Christ to understand that rather than streaming thoughts or words, we say to God, "Hallowed be Thy name." We learn we are kept in a place for oneness which by interpretation is in *the Name*.

> He replied, "I saw Satan fall like lightning from heaven. I have given you authority to trample on snakes and scorpions and to overcome all the power of the enemy; nothing will harm you. However, do not rejoice that the spirits submit to you, but rejoice that your names are written in heaven" (Luke 10:18–20, NIV).

Matthew Henry writes in his commentary on Matthew 6:9, "Hallowed be thy name" ... *we are directed to make the name of God our chief end; let all our petitions center in this and be regulated by it.*" "*When we pray that God's name may be glorified ...*

We make a virtue of necessity; for God will sanctify his own name, whether we desire it or not..." "I will be exalted among the heathen . . ." (Psalm 46:10, KJV).

Certainly the names of Jesus Christ and God the Father are the first occurrence of a relationship the Bible describes as oneness. The Name of God has keeping power, and this is very deep water indeed. As you lift your head to come close to God and do your business hallowing God's name, this is your opportunity to follow after God and His relationship with Christ. Their oneness begins out of your heart and is also for you—oneness.

Some of the above discussions may help you understand God's name, and I encourage you to study the Bible on your own and make the study of God's name one of your first studies. If you do not have a Bible, I would suggest you find the *Nelson Study Bible: New King James Version* (Thomas Nelson, 1997), and study the matter out.

Look online. Search websites like Crosswalk.com, BibleGateway.com, SearchGodsWord.org, and www.equip.org ("Christian Research Institute"), that is if you're not sure of the things pertaining to Jesus Christ, His church, and God the Father and His relationship to the Holy Spirit as He relates to humanity. There are many other good websites to choose from, including Catholic and messianic Jewish sources, but these are the few I resort to if my Logos Bible software does not contain my search criteria.

For the ones who may not or cannot get these resources to investigate God's wondrous and mighty Name, I have included a few comments from the study Bible,[34] commentaries, and a Bible dictionary:

NAMES OF GOD[35]—the titles or designations given to God throughout the Bible. In the ancient world, knowing another's name was a special privilege that offered access to that person's thought and life. God favored His people by revealing Himself by several names that offered special insight into His love and righteousness.

Jehovah/Yahweh. One of the most important names for God in the Old Testament is Yahweh, or Jehovah, from the verb "to be," meaning simply but profoundly, "He Is." His full name is found only in Exodus 3:14 and means "I am who I am" or "I will be who I will be." The four-letter Hebrew word YHWH was the name by which God revealed Himself to Moses at the burning bush. "I am who I am" signals the truth that nothing else defines who God is but God Himself. What He says and does is who He is.

The divine name Yahweh is usually translated "Lord" in English versions of the Bible, because it became a practice in late Old Testament Judaism not to pronounce the sacred name YHWH, but to say instead "my Lord" (*Adonai*)—a practice still used today in the synagogue. When the vowels of Adonai were attached to the consonants YHWH in the medieval period, the word Jehovah resulted. Today, many Christians use the word Yahweh, the more original pronunciation, not hesitating to name the divine name, since Jesus taught believers to speak in a familiar way to God.

From the same source, here are more names of the Lord in the Old Testament that stem from the basic name of Yahweh:

Jehovah-jireh. This name is translated as "The Lord Will Provide."

El. Another important root name for God in the Old Testament is El. By itself it refers to a god in the most general sense.

El Shaddai. Translated as "God Almighty," this name characterizes God as a source of blessing. It is the name with which God appeared to Abraham, Isaac, and Jacob (Exodus 6:3).

Elohim. This is the plural form of El, but it is usually translated in the singular. Elohim conveys the idea that the one supreme being, the only true God, is in some sense plural.

The following verses point us to God's Name and the Name of Christ. They help us know more about God's name if only from the shoreline. From a cursory first reading we learn; by study we are moved into deeper understanding of these spiritual dynamics.

> If you do not carefully observe all the words of this law that are written in this book, that you may fear this glorious and awesome name, THE LORD YOUR GOD (Deuteronomy 28:58).

> Then the priests, the sons of Levi, shall come near, for the Lord your God has chosen them to minister to Him and to bless in the *name of the Lord*; by their word every controversy and every assault shall be settled (Deuteronomy 21:5).

> Now set your heart and your soul to seek the Lord your God. Therefore arise and build the sanctuary of the

Lord God, to bring the ark of the covenant of the Lord and the holy articles of God into the house that is to be built for the *name of the Lord* (1 Chronicles 22:19).

And he said: "Naked I came from my mother's womb, And naked shall I return there. The Lord gave, and the Lord has taken away; Blessed be the *name of the Lord*" (Job 1:21).

Praise the Lord! Praise, O servants of the Lord, Praise the *name of the Lord*! Blessed be the *name of the Lord* From this time forth and forevermore! (Psalm 113:1–2).

Also the *sons of the foreigner* Who join themselves to the Lord, to serve Him, And to love the *name of the Lord*, to be His servants— *Everyone* who keeps from defiling the Sabbath, And holds fast My covenant—(Isaiah 56:6).

Surely the coastlands shall wait for Me; And the ships of Tarshish will come first, To bring your sons from afar, Their silver and their gold with them, To the *name of the Lord* your God, And to the *Holy One of Israel*, Because He has glorified you (Isaiah 60:9).

And it shall come to pass That whoever calls on the *name of the Lord* Shall be saved. For in Mount Zion and in Jerusalem there shall be deliverance, As the Lord has said, Among the remnant whom the Lord calls (Joel 2:32). Then the multitudes who went before and those who followed cried out, saying: "Hosanna to the Son of David! 'Blessed is He who comes in *the name of the Lord*!' Hosanna in the highest!" (Matthew 21:9)

And such were some of you. But you were washed, but you were sanctified, but you were justified in the name of the Lord Jesus and by the Spirit of our God (1 Corinthians 6:11).

Behold, I send an *Angel* before you to keep you in the way and to bring you into the place which I have prepared. Beware of Him and obey His voice; do not provoke Him, for He will not pardon your transgressions; for *My name is in Him*. But if you indeed obey His voice and do all that I speak, then I will be an enemy to your enemies and an adversary to your adversaries (Exodus 23:20–22).

For unto us a Child is born, Unto us a Son is given; And the government will be upon His shoulder. And *His name* will be called Wonderful, Counselor, Mighty God, Everlasting Father, Prince of Peace (Isaiah 9:6).

In His days Judah will be saved, And Israel will dwell safely; Now this *is His name* by which He will be called: THE LORD OUR RIGHTEOUSNESS (Jeremiah 23:6).

Therefore God also has highly exalted Him and given Him the *name which is above every name*, that at the *name of Jesus* every knee should bow, of those in heaven, and of those on earth, and of those under the earth, and that every tongue should confess that *Jesus Christ is Lord*, to the glory of God the Father (Philippians 2:9–11).

While you are praying intimately to God and your mind strays away from His name, when something breaks that focus, the above studies may help provide a way back into oneness with Christ. Study His Name often, and grow to understand what it means to you, for that is where you will climb back into the column of praise by the authority of His Holy name. "Hallowed be thy Name."

Having ... boldness to enter into the holiest by the blood of Jesus ... let us draw near with a true heart (Hebrews 10:19a, 22a).

Oh, the glory of the message! For fifteen centuries Israel had a sanctuary with a Holiest of All, into which, under pain of death, no one might enter. It's one witness was: Man cannot dwell in God's presence; cannot abide in His fellowship. And now how changed is all! As then the warning sounded: "No admittance! Enter not!" so now the call goes forth: "Enter in! The veil is rent; the Holiest is open; God waits to welcome you to His bosom; henceforth you are to live with Him." This is the message. Child! Thy Father longs for thee to enter, to dwell, and to go out no more forever. —Andrew Murray[36]

17

SUMMATION

To be commanded to love God in prayer, as Jesus taught us, is relational. This reestablishes fellowship, creature to Creator, lost in the garden of Eden through sin. The empowering experience of meeting with God each morning and evening transforms our thinking from out of the new heart. We experience God by the knowledge of spiritual sight and learn to draw from these events spiritual power to extend our hands into the marketplace to love our neighbor. When we fail at this, the Holy Spirit prompts us to review the acts of the day, that tomorrow we might have another opportunity to get it right, the opportunity to stand and say, "Thy kingdom come. Thy will be done in earth, as it is in heaven."

God's Son came within the virgin mother, Mary! His perfect life glorified God the Father and fulfilled Old Testament prophecy, the commandments, and the testimony. The iconographic tabernacle's speech is reforming text and church structures in our scientific age with the message that it is all about divine blood. There is no remission of sin without the shedding of blood, and Jesus Christ's blood within us, most assuredly, covers our head, our mercy seat, and we are able to relate to God again, as did Adam in the garden or as did Enoch, who walked with God. Empowered by such proximity, we are pleased to tell others of our friend Jesus, His love, power, and anointing blood upon our heads that from the place of the sealed heart we have recognition and relationship with the Father.

Ultimately, we have peered into these truths while detached in our own natural world, hoping to find the other place. This is the place where God is. All the foregoing pages must be viewed as an effort to get over to this other place. This book is about the transition, down to the lowly Christ Jesus from the natural place to participate in the spiritual place of oneness.

Whatever you may take away from this book, whatever scripture, story, or illustration helps move you closer to God, remember that it is first a transition downward to the resident Christ Jesus within you. Like a bucket cast into a well, the action presupposes the intent of bringing up the substance that is desired. God really is pleased by the effortful task of bringing up our gift. Holy is your Name, Father. He is also delighted that among so many of His children, it is you who bear this sacrificial gift from out of your heart.

Addendum 1
"ORTHODOX JEWS"

Many Gentile Christians believe they are at the end of the church age. They believe that they should be doing the business of preparing for one of the greatest prophetic events in history. Many believe the rapture of the church is that one final event! Many preachers today will openly state their belief that the next major event on the prophetic calendar is the rapture of Christians, the church of Jesus Christ. I must say that without the benefit of the interpretation of the material in this book and the Scripture we have just gone through, one could make such an assumption. For my part, I disagree with these evaluations concerning the time. There remains at least one prophetic event unfulfilled.

> Moses prophesied the event of which I speak, and it is recorded in the books of Deuteronomy and Romans: They have provoked Me to jealousy by *what* is not God;

They have moved Me to anger by their foolish idols. But I will provoke them to jealousy by those who are *not a nation*; I will move them to anger by a *foolish nation* (Deuteronomy 32:21).

Not a nation and a *foolish nation* may well apply to any nation of Moses' day not observing God's commands, statutes, and covenants. By observing this text, and the way it is used by Paul in the New Testament, we might argue that by application, the United States fits a *nation* that is *not a nation*—The USA is not a single ethnic people group, therefore not a nation.

In addition to the first part of the above scripture, the second part is now becoming most interesting. Have we not observed the direction that the liberal movements and the federal government have been taking the United States? I think we may now qualify as "*a foolish nation*," notice once more, a nation (foolish)—one that is practicing less and less allegiance to the God of Abraham, Isaac, and Jacob .

Moses says:

"I will provoke you to jealousy by those who are not a nation, I will move you to anger by a foolish nation" (Romans 10:19).

With the Bible claims revealed in this book and elsewhere, our understanding of the correct observations and interpretation of the tabernacle have their roots in the Gentile camp. This view, albeit from a sliver group of evangelicals, has essentially brought these views over into the Protestant Christian community. You can see how this might make the various Jewish communities angry and jealous of what we now possess (a working tabernacle) out of their own past. "I will move you to anger by a foolish nation."

Very long ago the Jewish race established, by its *types*, a relationship with God. They had, more or less, under their command God's vessel for moving close to Him upon a spiritual sea, the tabernacle/temple. After Titus destroyed the temple and temple worship in AD 70, most Jews believed they had lost the atoning instrument of mercy and thus they have been floundering for centuries for a way back to God. God, the designer of this vessel, has taken back control and turned the helm over to Christian believers who have been sealed with the blood of the Holy Christ.

Divinity has essentially taken possession of an abandoned ship at sea, by all legal rights. The way to God continues to be by way of blood sacrifice, no longer a *type* but a truth in fact. The way is cleared for Moses' and Paul's prophecy to be fulfilled. We shall find that the understanding and the proclaiming of these truths removes our last prophetic obstacle.

> The Deliverer will come out of Zion, And He will turn away ungodliness from Jacob; For this is My covenant with them, When I take away their sins (Romans 11:26–27).

Jesus Christ is come into believers by *Holy* blood smeared upon Jews, Gentile Protestants, and Catholics alike. When Jesus Christ shed His blood for our sin, by anticipation, God allowed the old Covenant and tabernacle/temple worship to continue simultaneous with his new covenant from Christ's death until

AD 70 when it finally ceased. The New Covenant replaced daily animal sacrifice upon a man-made altar while continuing to apply God's sacrifice upon the altar not made with hands. Our hearts are His throne room, therefore prophecy is fulfilled concerning "the throne of His Kingdom forever." (2 Samuel 7:12-13, Acts 15:16-17)

> According to the law almost all things are purified with blood, and without shedding of blood there is no remission (Hebrews 9:22).

For a few decades after the death of Jesus, God allowed the Jewish community to hear the message of the Messiah, the Christ, the one anointed from the *Holy*. The apostles gave freely the message of truth that God would not refuse to provide a way into His presence.

> This shall be a continual burnt offering throughout your generations at the door of the tabernacle of meeting before the Lord, where I will meet you to speak with you (Exodus 29:42).

Today we understand that Christ has come upon the altar, a lower region of the body, an *antitype* pointing us to the new heart. The eye that did not see has now come to see and behold the truth of the New Testament, which is the fulfillment of the Old Testament and the Pentateuch, the Mosaic law. His words are clear as we read: "Blindness in part has happened to Israel until the fullness of the Gentiles has come in. And so all Israel will be saved . . ." (Romans 11:25b–26a).

Because the Bible speaks the truth that "*no one comes unto the Father* except through [Jesus Christ]," the rabbinical prayers for atoning of sin—the Amadah—are never acknowledged by God. The sad reality is that most of our Jewish friends do not understand this truth. If they would just read and study these key elements in the Old Testament and the New Testament, they would find truth, and it would be clear to this chosen race. The Scripture tells us that though they call out to the God of Abraham, Isaac, and Jacob, He will not turn toward them!

> Jesus said to him, "*I am* the way, the truth, and the life. No one comes to the Father except through Me" (John 14:6).

Each soul, Jewish or otherwise, is potentially a rabbinical priest within the flesh, and must choose to accept Jesus' blood within and thereby allow the Holy Spirit to apply such blood to the old heart. With such blood sacrifice within, the priest (a *type* of our inner man) may now offer atonement daily, the spiritual smearing of blood upon the ark, upon the mercy seat, satisfying "a continual offering, morning and evening throughout your generations" (see Exodus 29:38-42). This sort of offering is for the daily cleaning of dirty hands and not to be confused with the one-time saving work of propitiation by atonement.

There is little doubt that the veil has been lifted from the eye that is now seeing. During the remaining days of the age of the Gentiles, great things are to come from the vows of those whose hearts care for the Jews. In the day that will follow the snatching away of Christian believers into the spirit realm, will Jews be cared for all the more, as their need will obviously be at its greatest? That should be our hope and prayer. Accordingly, we are told in Scripture that many, many Jewish brothers and sisters will still remain in ignorance of the Messiah.

We have come to see that a plan of God was unfolded, thanks to the wandering Israelites, whose plight depicted relationship with God through a temporary structure. This *type* of prophetic messenger is saying, "You must learn my lessons *before the silver cord is loosed*!" (see Ecclesiastes 12:6). While we observe Scripture, we also move from the rebellion of disobedience to loving God in a right relationship that says, "Love God with all your heart!" This is the correct application of the *shema* in the church age.

Loving Him is also taking the journey into the promised land of these temple experiences. We can know that using the tabernacle and the temple as a *type* increases our understanding of God's kingdom. We can participate in the New Covenant spiritually as we realize relationship with God and experience how it empowers our unique ministries. These physical manifestations of spiritual offices make sense to us if we see them as gatekeepers admitting the ones who have unlocked the code to the majesty of His name.

> *To the Chief Musician upon Gittith*
> (On the Instrument of Gath) –
> A Psalm of David (Psalm 8:1–9)

When I gaze into the night skies and see the work of Your fingers,
The moon and stars suspended in space.
What is man, that You are mindful of him?
You have given man a crown of glory and honor,

And have made him a little lower than the angels.
You have put him in charge of all creation:
The beasts of the field, the birds of the air, the fish of
   the sea.
But what is man that You are mindful of him?
O Lord, our God, the majesty and glory of Your name
Transcends the earth and fills the heavens.
O Lord, our God, little children praise You perfectly,
And so would we, and so would we. Alleluia, alleluia!
The majesty and glory of Your name. Alleluia, alleluia!
The majesty and glory of your name. Alleluia, Alleluia,
Alleluia, Alleluia, we praise your name!
Alleluia, Alleluia …

—Anthem, "The Majesty and Glory of Your Name," arranged
by Tom Fettke, YouTube.com search: The Majest and glory of
your name, Moody Church (start at 3 min, 30 seconds in).

Addendum 2

APOSTASY

Now the Spirit expressly says that in latter times some will depart from the faith, giving heed to deceiving spirits and doctrines of demons (1 Timothy 4:1).

Let no one deceive you by any means; for that Day will not come unless the falling away comes first (2 Thessalonians 2:3a).

They will turn their ears away from the truth, and be turned aside to fables (2 Timothy 4:4).

Apostasy has always troubled the Christian community, instilling doubt and lies and pulling the weak and undecided seeker from the ranks. The Great Apostasy, as the name suggests, is a much stronger form of heresy, and we may expect its influence to be strongest in the end of the church age. To be certain, we are experiencing such a time as the Bible describes, for it appears we are surrounded on all sides.

The Great Apostasy has come into our lives by way of human flesh and blood, and in most of the cases, the agent appears quite harmless. Deceiving spirits and demons influence these apostate laborers, and they are most assuredly our friends, relatives, co-workers, and others close to us. Are these people unaware of the influences affecting the world system by their hand?

One well-known group of such activists is located in Southern California. Although most of these followers would be characterized as "good people," Jesus Christ spoke with a ruler of His day about goodness, and we learn that not even Christians are good.

> "Good Teacher, what shall I do to inherit eternal life?"
> So Jesus said to him, "Why do you call Me good? No one is good but One, that is, God" (Luke 18:18–19).

These deceivers, including those deceived, in my opinion, are mostly unaware of the influence they have on others in the spiritual sense and how it withers the establishment of the kingdom of Jesus Christ. We have seen a mass flight away from the church. These searchers flee from the cross, and we are powerless to stop them even as we apply the tools of Christ's words of hope. Dead men like L. Ron Hubbard and his broken cistern, Scientology, as well as other similar cults, draw away the weak.

Most of these apostate groups are the modern-day movements that may have started with Madame Blavatsky and her society of Theosophists. These spiritual babes are lost searchers drawn off by wolves, who for their part may receive condemnation and the wrath of God.

For God so loved the world that He gave His only begotten Son, that whoever believes in Him should not perish but have everlasting life (John 3:16).

The Buddhists, Zen practitioners, and contemplation groups who look within the heart without the benefit of the blood of Jesus Christ have always been thought of as seekers of truth. Love of others seems to be at the center of their peaceful pursuit of harmony, peace and brotherly love and while spiritual consciousness is certain, the benefits remain in question. A spiritual link with a spiritual world is a good thing, but which world, and in which direction will it take the seeker?

We have learned that God directs our attention upward and builds upon a heavenly kingdom. We need to ask "in which direction" do these groups influence the seeker to move? In these latter days, the Bible tells us, "some will depart from the faith," and will it be for building up or tearing down or—worst of all—a neutral void, falling into the pit of the bowels, into a black hole of nothingness?—like a senseless pursuit of a blank stare, which will do little except take these seekers further from life in Christ. The fear of eternal damnation and separation from God helps to conform the Christian practitioner, while the occult wanderer is not drawn away into hellish behavior but rather a false sense of peace and joy, having found the metaphysical illusion of inner oneness with the self.

Loving God with all one's heart is not loving the god within the heart, your contemplative self! If you are to look into the heart, Christ's blood must be there to guide you upward and into relationship with God. We are not good men and women by virtue of this blood; we are perfectly holy men and women by this blood and able to love others by God's accepting us and empowering our ministry goals (Hebrews 10:1, 14: "The law . . . can never . . . make those who approach perfect . . . For by one offering He has perfected forever those who are being sanctified.")

Loving God begins here with biblical truth, and its fruit becomes abilities and avenues for loving others in God's power. We love them by sharing the abiding oneness we have by this blood. God has made this possible through a *Holy* Christ, so that by the sharing in testimony of Jesus' life, truth will come alive to a world lost in apostasy.

Sitting in the void of contemplation does not empower us with relationship with God, nor does it prepare us to illuminate others; it empowers a peaceful nothingness. Seeking the inner self darkens the mind and opens a spirit world in this realm without the hope of the eternal kingdom of God to come within us and, by this pathway, come into others.

All the years of practicing these fallen arts with such temporary rewards should cause these seekers to look with enthusiasm and hope upon the structure of the tabernacle. Yes, there is the message of Life within the heart, the true "Light of the world." It is Jesus they will find in these pages. He is hope, life, and purpose and brings His reward with Him—not a void or vacuum but the joy of the Lord and the peace of God. He wants to enliven your practice of seeking truth by offering you forgiveness from the sin of omission, rejecting His only Son, by propitiation, the atoning for sin. He will come into your heart and set you right and on the pathway to life here and away in the eternal place. His calling is for you to return to the one true God, who loves you with an everlasting Love.

None of the ancient mystics but one rose from the grave. His body never saw corruption, nor could death hold Him down. "His soul was not left in Hades, nor did His flesh see corruption" (Acts 2:31). Over five hundred witnesses were there and shall be in heaven for cross-examination, who saw the *Holy* Christ ascend to the heavens many days after His death upon a Roman cross.

This is the One and only hope of the New Age seeker. Come, come over here and see where He is staying; it is not far from the place where you go to look for truth. You look into the *hara*, the belly, the focal point and the place from where you climb up the other way.

> Most assuredly, I say to you, he who does not enter the sheepfold by the door, but climbs up some other way, the same is a thief and a robber (John 10:1).

Come up and into a place Jesus has prepared for His own, the mansion He has prepared for you (see John 14:2). This mansion Christians speak of may actually refer to a room wherein you have sought out the peace which has eluded you. You enter this room alone, without guidance or authority, as an intruder. In the Bible, God refers to His plan as a yoke: "My yoke is easy" (Matthew 11:30). Come in and follow Him; this Jesus is calling out for you to come this way.

Not only is His way easy for seekers like you, but there is spiritual power in this way. God's Holy Spirit is alive and active in the life of the followers of Jesus Christ, and He releases this power into the life of the ones He trusts. One of the benefits of the new life is the Bible—for illumination of truth and power for its application, which is the true secret of joy and purpose: giving yourself by this power to others for true life in Him.

You may be advanced in the arts of spiritual perception, and you may have had some understanding moments. Yet I daresay your quest has been empty of lasting peace and joy. I can presume this because of my own experiences in this discipline many years ago. You and your fellow inward gazers have seen about all there is to see after barren years of looking within. You watch each other in hopes of finding the next path to purpose that will not fail.

I challenge you to come over here and see where Christ Jesus is staying, so that His true spiritual power may help you across the great divide. Do you think about the ones you may have influenced? Some of those lost in the apostasy may well be your responsibility, and I charge you with the quality of their eternal existence if the exhortation is appropriately placed.

Will you choose for them, choose where they will spend eternity? It is almost certain that you hear and understand this call better than they. Come along inward as He made you to come, and find Peace and Joy in Christ Jesus for lasting purpose. Then together we may hope to reclaim those that are lost (Luke 15:4; 19:10).

Jesus is the name given to Him by the Father, the name above all names. He is the Lamb, the bright and morning star. The one who is called Jesus Christ, it is Him—by His blood—who wants to come into your heart, *hara*, or belly and come in today if you will take His free gift of life. All you need do is to say these words from your heart and mean them:

1. I have sinned, and I turn from this life of sin.
2. I accept Jesus Christ, His blood sacrifice, as cleansing of my sin.

3. I choose to invite Him into my heart (*hara*) by my faith.

If you have prayed this simple prayer and believe in its truth, you are saved and will live eternally with Jesus Christ. Here are some of the responsibilities of this commitment:

- Get a Bible and start reading it every day!
- Find a good church—Calvary Chapel, Evangelical Free Church, Baptist, among others.
- If you were raised Catholic, than go to mass, *read the Bible*, attend study groups, and fellowship with others who have made the same decision.
- Take part in fellowship in the church weekly.
- Join a Bible study, preferably gender specific.
- Talk to God, as in the above material...pray.
- Congratulations, and welcome to the family of God.

Addendum 3

PHYSICAL, SPIRITUAL, & OTHER CONSIDERATIONS

The Physical

The physical posture of standing and praying is by all means recommended but not a mandatory discipline. Initially, one might find slight balance problems from standing and praying, either from one's feet being on an uneven floor, grains of sand underfoot, or bulges in socks. The idea is to focus on the task; thoughts other than one's location, or the mere novelty of standing while praying, must be overcome as distractions.

The feet should be spaced shoulder-width apart. Whether or not you wear shoes should be irrelevant. The torso should be straight, even if the trunk is bent slightly forward. (You might find that your gluteus maximus protrudes a bit, improving balance.) The shoulders also should be straight: one will find more comfort in the long run if one has as straight a posture as possible.

The arms can hang down, but you will find that the hands lifting in praise will bring the arms up slightly. A common practice is to rotate the palms upward or to the side, and they will eventually have a sense of heaviness about them. This may be the influence of the Holy Spirit as He directs His spiritual control through these resources and over the physical aspects of abiding for praise, worship, and ultimately empowering ministry.

The head should naturally tilt upward. If you find yourself looking at the floor, you may need to refocus on the God who has called us to heaven. The eyes can be open or closed—you might at first want to close the eyes to shut out distractions: over time, you should acquire the ability to mentally focus on the Father's name, through the Holy Spirit, while looking up and abiding in Christ to the exclusion of all else.

Sometimes you may experience rapid breathing, having begun your session with deep breathing in your own strength. You should remember that this phenomenon is expected, and raising your own level of breathing is viewed as a helpful aid rather than an artificial method toward abiding oneness. You might involuntarily utter some sounds, audibly germane to intimate worship and praise. As any good battle goes, physical intensity is expected, and noises out of the spiritual experience should be unique to this practice—a source of encouragement as you overcome the opposition.

THE SPIRITUAL

During worship, the mind usually is what first engages the attention, ignores distractions, and directs the other events. The mind is very much engaged in the procession into oneness in contrast to the blankness of the new-age mystical mind. Your mind will begin to lessen its involvement from 100 percent down to about 20 percent, while participation of your heart increases from zero to about 80 percent. Of course, these numbers should be understood as arbitrary and illustrative. The mind is not completely turned off so much as it is subject to Christ and His purposes of Holy Spiritual guidance. The Holy Spirit is showing us the condition of oneness in Christ to the exclusion of a *streaming* mind. Prayer—hallowing God's name focused out of the heart, is what loves God and worships "of the Son" (Revelation 22:1) in proper proportions: the heart ascendant over the private praying mind.

Both Old and New Testaments use the internal organs as *types* of this spiritual activity. In many cases in the Old Testament, the "heart" was understood to be the mind. The bowels were the seat of affections. Thus, Jesus says later that, "Out of [the] bowels will come rivers of living water" (John 7:38), later understood as referring to the Holy Spirit. In worship, you will find God increasing your love for Jesus and then for others, and derive many blessings from the "bowels," the seat of your affections. Our wants and desires are what we lay on the "brazen altar" when we worship God. In our heart and mind, these wants and desires belong to Him. As we put God's Son first, God's Spirit makes our spirit grow in the knowledge of abiding oneness, and this is how our wants and desires become His.

The mind's work is to keep the spirit in worship and prayer through Christ Jesus (ignoring distractions, directing one's prayers) by the Holy Spirit, whether or not the emotions cooperate. Actually, in time, one's emotions will cooperate. But do expect Satan to try to use them against you, at least at first.

In private prayer, one of the important jobs of the mind is to block distractions and hindrances from worshiping God and then to *refocus* with Him who saved us from our sins. We should expect the Holy Spirit to help us maintain this focus by faith in Him who comforts us. These are the desires of Christ who has declared the Holy Spirit to be our helper. The mind functions best during worship as the tool of the heart to focus, protect, and direct the abiding state. This is what the mind does as it asserts control of praying the Disciple's Prayer (Matthew 6:9–13). While the mind is ever presenting the tenets of the prayer, the heart is what *does* the prayer. Then one acquires an abiding sense of active praise, a moving, surging fountain of praise to our Creator like the silver cord of old.

> *Remember your Creator* before the silver cord is loosed.
> Or the golden bowl is broken,
> Or the pitcher shattered at the fountain,
> Or the wheel broken at the well (Ecclesiastes 12:6).

Other Considerations

The twenty-first-century American has a peculiar fear of being alone. By *peculiar* I mean that people don't mind being alone if they have control over when, where, and how such a condition occurs. We are here talking about *choosing* to be alone with God, without backup or help in worshiping God, except for that help offered spiritually by the Comforter. We are talking about the "prayer closet" where Jesus directed us to be alone with God.

Reading is a skill that we must work at learning. Once it is learned, however, we come to enjoy reading. Worshiping our Creator is an activity we study to learn because, once we have learned, we will enjoy worshiping God in the Son through the

Holy Spirit. There actually is a fellowship with God that is so full of the Holy Spiritual presence of Christ within us that His intensity can feel as if a switch has been opened for ecstasy to flow. But the switch isn't from "off" to "on" as much as it is from being "out of" pasture to being "in" pasture. By faith we are sealed within by Christ's blood, this hope, this condition exists within each Christian. These dynamics are just waiting to be actuated from the top down demonstrating our God in Christ always knows us and has chosen to love us in the flesh.

When we choose to pray privately, we choose to participate in this supernatural relationship and we are strengthened by our awareness that it is by Jesus Christ's blood that God is made available to sinful men and women. How else might a fallen world raise itself in oneness each morning and evening to grow stronger and to become at home in His glory.

The acronym ACTS (Adoration, Confession, Thanksgiving, and Supplication) isn't so much a prayer method among many methods or a protocol which man has implemented. Rather it is a trail toward God that is seldom traveled well and is fraught with opposition. This method, while presenting a model to contain and discipline prayer progress, actually expands the opening of a pathway into the mind by thoughts, ideas, and experiences from the world and its systems. Satan has access to this process of prayer formation, and because the power of Scripture is seldom present in the average seeker, the enemy has his way with us.

Learning to become intimate with God, especially in the earliest stages, is very troublesome if you are not committed to see the practice through its difficult stages of doubt and Satanic mischief. While we believe we are progressing, often we have fallen into a void of looking inward at the latest concern in our lives or simply into the self. Focus upward and on loving God by prayer proposed for His adoration, and you won't run the risk of finding yourself emerging from yet another set of lost moments with your beautiful heavenly Father and His wonderful Son. We look back into such side trails that represented what is commonly referred to as a daydream, and wonder how long we were gone away in follies!

Starting off well has always been the intention of the ones using acronyms of this sort, yet the ends are the same if Scripture isn't the basis of intimate worship of God from the heart with good focus and discipline from the mind. I like the Lord's prayer. Scripture is the basis of the power of the Holy Spirit, and He both knows where heaven is and can take us there Himself by these means. He loves to use Jesus' words to accomplish His duties; this is how the Holy Spirit glorifies Christ and determines our pathway to heaven through the abiding Christ. The Holy Spirit intends to strengthen us, both to worship and to witness. Lately, such strength is subsiding and may become rare amid the churches as they move away from Scripture and the blood of Christ into a one-world system.

Simply standing in abiding oneness with God can seem like the height of passivity. What does it accomplish? We do not visit our friends to accomplish something, and likewise we do not worship God to accomplish something. Pagans think that way. The one who trusts Jesus Christ for salvation merely wants to fellowship with Christ and worship the Father as He commanded because He is worthy to be worshiped. Since when is fellowship with God a waste of time? Rather, there is nothing on this planet that is more important. Fellowship with our Creator is exactly why He created us. When we are "in" Christ and come into pasture, our focus shifts from what we might have come for, to praising God and making *Holy* His Name.

It's not that the road has no obstacles, but that being in the Holy Spirit is confirmation of being on the right road. As Nehemiah learned, any time God's people say, "Let us rise and build," Satan says, "Let us rise and oppose." Since Satan is already defeated, we should ignore him, along with the distractions, problems, and obstacles he puts in the road to fellowship.

There are places one can go to obtain quiet and solitude with God. Sometimes, that place will be into the stillness of the heart, a place built by an internal ability to focus wholly on the God of the universe to the utter exclusion of anything else. Most people, however, haven't this ability (yet) and must have help in attaining an external quiet.

With over six and a half billion people on this planet, the first distraction is likely to be our fellow humans. And our initial witness to them can be that we need to be alone with God at this time, for this hour. This is, perhaps, the single most important thing that we can do for our family: declare by actions—not words—the importance of stopping and listening to God.

Jesus well knew the minimal space that poverty affords. However, He told us how to pray, and that such prayer must be "in spirit and in truth" (John 4:4). Truly, we can stand in our clothes closet and be able to enter God's throne room. In fact, this is the only "dimension travel" humans will ever accomplish, and it is the privilege of God's children only.

One of the stronger temptations in prayer is to go outside amid nature. We should be spending time with the Creator, not His creation. To emphasize spiritual fellowship, we should be working to minimize the physical distractions, of which nature has very many, from temperature variations to insects. That nature is only a series of distractions from God is another reason why Jesus told us about merely standing in a closet.

If we are in a room, others, creating additional distractions, can enter that room. As noted above, others can be asked politely to leave us alone for an hour. For our own sake *and* for others' sake, we should try to be inaccessible for that time, and closets accomplish this well enough. Some might have no closets at all. Often the only answer is to then turn the room into a "closet" and, again, ask to be left alone for an hour.

Addendum 4

THINGS TO DO AND NOT TO DO

THINGS TO DO

1. Ask the Holy Spirit, before your session, to show you Christ Jesus within and ask His help to pray to the Father. In John 14:14 Jesus says, "If you ask anything in My name, I will do it."
2. Before your session, thank the Father for His Son and His blood sacrifice. Thank Him also for the Holy Spirit's help.
3. What we ask, we assume we have by faith. Ask, and then move on in belief.
4. A spiritual metaphor could be the center lamp, "radiant light "burning bright.
5. Ask the Son: "Help me; I will be praying the prayer You taught Your disciples to pray."
6. Remember that your prayer is an action within a living spiritual column, the tabernacle.
7. Also, remember to fast often, at least every few months, for spiritual lift.

8. Don't become frustrated, worried, or anxious; that is not of God. Rather, be joyous to be learning how you are made to enter "*in.*"
9. Deep breathing by the nose helps the mouth stay moist and lifts the heart.

While standing and praying

1. Focus on *doing* mostly the first section of the prayer: "Our Father, hallowed be thy name." You might want to pause in *wonder* at the "our" in your heart.
2. "Our" is something two entities act out of. Understand that, "it is you and Christ Jesus" who are praising, using Holy Scripture that God loves to hear.
3. Do the holy giving of yourself within this framework, by Christ really "in" you!
4. A *calm, letting go, relaxing sensation* should be sought in the lower extremities of your heart or bowels. Holy Spiritual attachment of your spirit (small *s*) takes place here.
5. A fountain moves upward, and Christ Jesus, by the Holy Spirit, knows the way. Praise moves up, and you should *always* focus the mind to participate in this phenomenon. The mind directs the heart to work this out!
6. Look up, look into God's name, and Holy Him. It's a command and is not a process of evaluation. Refocusing on *God's name* should be constant in the early weeks and months.
7. Look up at God and "Holy" Him, converting Matthew 6:9–13, just the first ten words, into streaming sentiment for most of the prayer; visit the other parts of this prayer for 20 percent of the time or less.

8. Expect your hands to become heavy, fall and rise. They may fall when praise is blocked or grow still when you start thinking; they may rise up when you're abiding or while you're praising, or they may stay to your sides.
9. Holy Him, and sense power moving out, upward toward Him in rivers of spirituality.
10. Enjoy standing. As the eagle flies, the Holy Spirit will control your body in perfection.
11. Expect rapid breathing to feed your Holy prayer passion. Working and battling require an intensity of effort exclusive to this activity.
12. Do expect your mind to wander, but resist. Mental thinking takes one out of pasture. Resist, and focus at the center lamp base, in the blood; and look to God.
13. A wandering mind, absent of abiding oneness, can be corrected by Psalm 86:12: "I will praise You, O Lord . . . ," understanding that God can be mindful of your efforts, and at this moment there are not many praising people struggling through the enemy's ranks to love God.
14. The Spirit of Holiness moves with you, upon such faithful declarations, and joins you to help (see Romans 8:26–27).
15. Do five to ten minutes of praise each day, aiming toward forty-five minutes to an hour as a goal.
16. A fountain moves upward, and Christ Jesus within will do the same. Praise moves up, and you should *always* focus the mind on this phenomenon.
17. Start by looking up into the place of God's habitation. It is hard to stay connected. Focus on His name, refocus on Him, now refocus, and praise. (You may have to refocus. :-)

18. Exercise your focus up onto God's name, looking into His name until you become stronger. You should be able to sustain longer sessions in this way.
19. "He dwells with you and *will be in you*" (John 14:17) should be understood as the Holy Spirit "with you" (second things) and "in you" (first things). The hands lifting in praise are "with you," a sort of second things.

Things Not to Do

1. Don't worry about physical posture; it will come in time. If you're looking to correct posture, you're not praising God. Be still and know—!
2. Don't ask yourself: " Am I doing this …?" "Is this working …?" Looking for evidence of the effects is not abiding by faith. Doing "Holy is your name" is walking by faith.
3. Don't think so much. Look for your heart, and give it dominion. Christ Jesus waits for you here!
4. Don't look for substance: visions, shadows, or images. These are not relevant to faith.
5. Don't expect to work in the spiritual realm alone. Christ dwells here, and it is a partnership of you, Christ, and the Holy Spirit. Keep at it, and He will pick you up.
6. Don't thrust your hands up and above your head, it's tiresome. Rather, practice keeping the elbows bent and the hands six to eight inches from the corners of your eyes. Lower them as needed; worship is spiritual, and the power in the hands can bless the Lord out of your heart. It's what comes out of you that will reach into heaven!
7. Don't think that, because torrents of holy praise are not happening today, something is wrong. Each session with Him is His gift to you, and each one is different.

8. Don't always keep your eyes closed. Alternate if you need to, working toward open eyes.
9. Don't expect these sessions to be quiet. Groaning and breathing noises are common.
10. Don't forget to ask the Holy Spirit to remind you to look right at God, to refocus your wandering mind upon His glorious name.
11. Don't forget that a fountain moves upward. Yours will do the same. Praise moves up, and you should always focus the mind on recognizing this phenomenon.
12. Don't miss out on a single day of fellowship with God, in Christ. Such days are lost for all time.
13. Don't give up. The enemy has disguised your rights to heaven in many ways; chief among them is despair. Persist from the heart up toward the face of God.
14. Find a partner to hold you accountable. "… it's not what we expect that gets done, it's what we inspect that prevails."

Addendum 5

PROPHECY

Prophetic speech, or speaking correctively by the divine will of God toward the needs of the church is usually actuated by notions of errant administration of the Biblical Commandments, Statutes, and the Testimony.

Those found in proximity to God, in intimate prayer and praise, are the ones most likely hearing from Him and are compelled to speak out. These are the ones abiding in fellowship through Christ, who also balance their time in Bible reading and study.

First, if a prophetic message is to glorify God, It must clarify doctrine and errant church structures. Secondly, the speech must harmonize with the accepted teachings of the Bible. Since prophets are subject to prophets, in other words, because they are responsible for their own right behavior within the context of a loving, nurturing church, and that one's own self-consciousness, self-command is never lost, it is best if prophets remember to utilize:

SCRIPTURE
Having then gifts differing according to the grace that is given to us, *let us use them:* if prophecy *let us prophesy* in proportion to our faith (Romans 12:6)…"

COMMENTARY

"Teaching (is) aimed at the understanding." "Exhortation (is) aimed at the heart and will." Prophecy can be defined as: *exhortation.*

Both words are in the locative of sphere, the idea being that the one who is given a teaching gift should remain within the exercise of that gift, and the one who has been given the gift of exhortation, within the exercise of that gift. Wuest, K. S. (Rom. 12:6)

Two things are combined to make the prophet: an insight granted by God into the divine secrets or mysteries, and a communication to others of these secrets. It includes the concept of divine grace, but with the warnings, announcements of judgment, and so forth… In the case of the OT, the prophets' preaching was a foretelling of the salvation yet to be accomplished. In the NT, prophecy was a publication of the salvation already accomplished, insofar as it did not concern itself with realities still future (Zodhiates).

Addendum 6

HALLOW

"... *hagiazo* /hag·ee·ad·zo/AV translates as "sanctify" 26 times, "hallow" twice, and "be holy" once. 1) to render or acknowledge, or to be venerable or hallow. 2) to separate from profane things and dedicate to God. 2a consecrate things to God (Strong, J.)."

The Bible reminds us of where we are to place God in our lives. Deuteronomy 5:6-7 the first of His commandments:

1. I am the Lord thy God...
2. Thou shalt have no other Gods before me.

I am the Lord ... and Have no little gods or distraction before me is looking, attending to, and focusing on God alone. Where is our help for doing this?

Consider that, while in prayer, we do not require protection from flesh and bones but protection from evil: "keep them from the evil one" (John 17:15). Power for abiding is in the Name, and we are helped by this supplication from Christ's words to understand that rather than streaming thoughts or words, we say to God, "Hallowed be Thy name." We learn we are kept in a place for oneness which by interpretation is in the Name.

When we pray, we need to be sure to avoid repeating words instead of doing what the word says: "hallow God's name." We can do this once we learn that speech is but one form of relating the message.

> After this manner therefore pray ye: Our Father which art in heaven, Hallowed be thy name. —Matt. 6:6

This practice requires faith for the purpose of hallowing God out of your heart. It's an upward sensation, of the thing you are doing; remember, you are doing something, and that something is streaming the sentiment of "hallowed be thy name"! Your offering is not just a sentence in this prayer but the substance out of the kingdom, which has come into you.

Addendum 7

ANOINTING

I. Howard Marshal discusses Anointing (1 John 2:20):

". . . Gnostics laid claim to a special anointing not shared by other Christians. However, we have no definite evidence of this practice in the first century, and the fact that Paul uses the metaphor independently speaks against John's having derived the idea from the practices of his opponents.

A different understanding of the metaphor was introduced to English readers by C. H. Dodd. He argued that the anointing (*oil*) refers to the Word of God which teaches the truth to believers and which is objective in its testimony to the truth. Because they have received the Word of God, the true believers have come to know the truth, and therefore they have the antidote to false teaching . . . " (italic emphasis added pointing out that *oil* is not in the original)

". . . Further, the thought of teaching by the 'anointing' (v. 27) fits in nicely with the identification of the anointing as the Word of God. Finally, John says that the anointing remains in his readers in the same way as he speaks about the Word of God or the truth remaining in them (1 Jn. 2:14; 2 Jn. 2). All this adds up to a strong case that the anointing is to be identified with the Word of God. Above all, when understood in this way, John's statement is free from the danger of subjectivism. The false teachers could lay claim to spiritual illumination: how, then, could

John's readers know for sure that their spiritual experience was of superior quality? If it is simply a matter of comparing claims to spiritual illumination, one person's claim may be as good as another's. But if John rests his case on his readers' possession of the objective testimony of the Word of God, as handed down in the church, then clearly his case rests on a solid foundation.

Nevertheless, it remains difficult to think of the Word of God, handed down and preached in the church, as being described under the metaphor of anointing. Moreover, the parallels which we saw between what is said here about the anointing and what is said in John 14–16 about the Spirit cannot be simply laid aside. Consequently, we should probably take the step of combining the two interpretations of our passage. The anointing is the Word taught to converts before their baptism and apprehended by them through the work of the Spirit in their hearts (cf. 1 Thess. 1:5f.). This view has been cogently presented by I. de la Potterie, who sums up: 'The anointing is indeed God's word, not as it is preached externally in the community, but as it is received by faith into men's hearts and remains active, thanks to the work of the Spirit.'

This gives a satisfying view of the passage. The antidote to false teaching is the inward that reception of the Word of God, administered and confirmed by the work of the Spirit."

Authors observations:
The above two competing views are best understood when they are coordinated out of the mission of Christ, and His blood covering. The Unguent is our access to God, cleaning the conscience, thereby enabling joyous sessions of abiding in oneness with God—regardless of sin's stain (1 John 3:21). Many textual experts assume the Holy Spirit is this anointing. Yet the president for this anointing, in the Old Testament, was applied to

recipients but once. Today, this bloody unguent which cleans and covers our conscience, remains a daily practice for Christians. The Blood of Christ, the "one body" of believers, is about abiding oneness. " . . . I was in the Spirit on the Lords day . . . " (Rev.1:10), presumably a place John went often and thus, he was teaching his followers about their spiritual birth into Gods presence, here and in 1 John 2:29!

While looking for intellectual solutions, it is easy to forget context—even for scholarly exegetics'. The blood of Christ, and propitiation for sin (1 Jn. 2:1-2), is the correct context. Comparing Greek morphology (word formation), and syntax (sentence formation), may yield helpful results in understanding John's intent; and while scholars wrestle with the meaning of anointing—"Blood, Spirit, or the Word"—all show similar morphology (Noun, Neuter, Singular, and Accusative). So, here, the Greek is unfruitful.

The context of 1 John 1, 2, and 3, is sin and its aberrant growth impacting the communities John is instructing. This is key to understanding Blood as primary to our anointing. Consider: Chapter 1, "All sin." Chapter 2, "Christ our advocate" when we do sin. Chapter 3, "Sinlessness" through abiding oneness. The "Spirit" and the "Word" clearly participate in the work of making sinful men—holy. Yet, as in the Old, God requires a blood sacrifice for the remission of sin, and abiding fellowship. The interpretation that says, the Holy Spirit is our anointing, is not primary in John's mind, and so, the Holy Spirit must wait a few verses later for a valid introduction (1 John 3:24).

"But you have an anointing from the Holy One, and you know all things" (1 John 2:20). Put simply: Knowing God in oneness is "knowing all things." What "*I* know in part," regardless of the Holy Spirit, is but a part of knowing all things (1 Co. 13:12b).

BIBLIOGRAPHY

Chambers, Oswald. *My Utmost for His Highest: Selections for the Year.* Grand Rapids, MI. Discovery House Publishers, 1993, 1935.

Lovelace, Richard. *Dynamics of Spiritual Life, An Evangelical Theology of Renewal,* Downers Grove, IL: InterVarsity Press, 1979. email@ivpress.com, email@ivpress.com? subject=InterVarsity%20Press

Schaeffer, Francis August. *True Spirituality.* Tyndale House Publishers, Inc., 1971

Tozer, A.W. *The Pursuit of God,* copyright 1948, 1982, 1993, by Zur Ltd. Used by permission of WingSpread Publishers, a division of Zur Ltd.

Vincent's Word Studies in the New Testament, Hendrickson Publications, Inc. Peabody, Massachusetts. August 2009

The following Libronix Digital Library System, along with its listed title, are electronic editions, used by permission of Libronix Digital Library System, Libronix Corporation, 1313 Commercial Street, Bellingham, WA. 98225-4372 Logos Bible Software: Libronix Corporation. http://www.libronix.com:

Carson, D. A. (1994). *New Bible commentary: 21st century edition* (4th ed.). Leicester, England; Downers Grove, Ill., USA: Inter-Varsity Press.

Ferguson, Sinclair B., and J. I. Packer. *New Dictionary of Theology.* Downers Grove, IL: InterVarsity Press, 2000, c1988.

Hardman, S. G. and D. L. Moody, *Thoughts for the Quiet Hour* (April 19), Willow Grove, PA: Woodlawn Electronic Publishing, 1998. Originally published by Revell (Chicago), 1990.

Henry, Matthew *Matthew Henry's Commentary on the Whole Bible: Complete and Unabridged in One Volume.* Peabody: Hendrickson, 1996, 1991.

Heritage of great evangelical teaching: Featuring the best of Martin Luther, John Wesley, Dwight L. Moody, C.H. Spurgeon and others. 1997, c1996 (electronic ed.). Logos Library Systems. Nashville: Thomas Nelson.

Hodge, C. (1997). *Systematic theology.* Oak Harbor, WA: Logos Research Systems, Inc.

Karleen, P. S. (1987). *The handbook to Bible study: With a guide to the Scofield study system.* New York: Oxford University Press.

Kempis, Thomas à. *The Imitation of Christ*, (1996) Oak Harbor, WA: Logos Research Systems.

Kittel, G., Friedrich, G., & Bromiley, G. W. (1995, c1985). *Theological dictionary of the New Testament*. Translation of: *Theologisches Worterbuch zum Neuen Testament*. (581). Grand Rapids, Mich.: W.B. Eerdmans.

Louw, J. P., & Nida, E. A. (1996, c1989). *Greek-English lexicon of the New Testament:* Based on semantic domains. (1:728). New York: United Bible societies. Electronic ed. of the 2nd edition.

MacArthur, John (*Matthew*) Chicago: Moody Press, 1989.

Marshall, I. Howard, *The Epistles of John*. © 1978 Grand Rapids, Mich.: Wm. B. Eerdmans

Nestle, E., & McReynolds, P. R. (1997, c1982). *Nestle Aland 26th Edition Greek New Testament with McReynolds English Interlinear*. Oak Harbor: Logos Research Systems, Inc.

Robertson, A. (1997). *Word Pictures in the New Testament*. Vol.V c1932, Vol. VI c1933 by Sunday School Board of the Southern Baptist Convention. (Jn 6:56). Oak Harbor: Logos Research Systems.

Stanley, Charles F., Logos Library Systems, *The Glorious Journey* Nashville, TN: Thomas Nelson, 1997, 1996.

Strong, J. (1996). *The exhaustive concordance of the Bible* : Showing every word of the test of the common English version of the canonical books, and every occurrence of each word in regular order. Ontario: Woodside Bible Fellowship.

Thomas Nelson, *The Holy Bible, New King James Version*. 1982. Nashville, TN

The Holy Bible : King James Version. 1995 (1769 edition of the 1611 Authorized Version.) Bellingham WA: Logos Research Systems, Inc.

Walvoord, J. F., Zuck, R. B., & Dallas Theological Seminary. (1983-c1985). *The Bible Knowledge commentary : An exposition of the scriptures*. Wheaton, IL: Victor Books.

Wuest, Kenneth S. *Wuest's Word Studies from the Greek New Testament: For the English Reader*. Grand Rapids: Eerdmans, 1997, 1984. Electronic ed. Logos Library Systems.

Youngblood, R. F. *Nelson's New Illustrated Dictionary*. Nashville: Thomas Nelson, 1995.

Zodhiates, S. (2000, c1992, c1993). *The complete word study dictionary*: New Testament (electronic ed.) (G3306). Chattanooga, TN: AMG Publishers.

NOTES

1. Strong, J. (1996). The exhaustive concordance of the Bible : Showing every word of the text of the common English version of the canonical books, and every occurrence of each word in regular order. (electronic ed.) (G5545). Ontario: Woodside Bible Fellowship
2. Wuest, K. S. (1997, c1984). Wuest's word studies from the Greek New Testament: For the English reader (1 Jn 2:20). Grand Rapids: Eerdmans (emphasis added).
3. Louw, J. P., & Nida, E. A. (1996, c1989). Greek-English lexicon of the New Testament: Based on semantic domains (electronic ed. of the 2nd edition.) (1:219). New York: United Bible societies.
4. Zodhiates, S. (2000, c1992, c1993). The complete word study dictionary: New Testament (electronic ed.) (G2983). Chattanooga, TN: AMG Publishers.
5. Louw, J. P., & Nida, E. A. (1996, c1989). Greek-English lexicon of the New Testament: Based on semantic domains (electronic ed. of the 2nd edition.) (1:793). New York United Bible societies.
6. Walvoord, J. F., Zuck, R. B., & Dallas Theological Seminary. (1983-c1985). The Bible knowledge commentary: An exposition of the scriptures (2:297). Wheaton, IL: Victor Books. (emphasis in original, Dash is added)
7. Zodhiates, S. (2000, c1992, c1993). The complete word study dictionary: New Testament (electronic ed.) (G3306). Chattanooga, TN: AMG Publishers.
8. Kittel, G., Friedrich, G., & Bromiley, G. W. (1995, c1985). Theological dictionary of the New Testament. Translation of: Theologisches Worterbuch zum Neuen Testament. (581). Grand Rapids, Mich.: W.B. Eerdmans.
9. Louw, J. P., & Nida, E. A. (1996, c1989). Greek-English lexicon of the New Testament : Based on semantic domains (ed. of the 2nd edition.) (1:728). New York: United Bible societies.
10. Robertson, A. (1997). Word Pictures in the New Testament. Vol.V c1932, Vol.VI c1933 by Sunday School Board of the Southern Baptist Convention. (Jn 6:56). Oak Harbor: Logos Research Systems.
11. *The Handbook to Bible Study* (1987) *With a guide to the Scofield study system.* New York: Oxford University Press. *The Importance of Literary Features in the Book of Revelation*
12. *Nelson's New Illustrated Dictionary.* Nashville: Thomas Nelson, 1995.
13. *Wuest's Word Studies from the Greek New Testament* Grand Rapids: Eerdmans, 1984. (emphases in original)
14. Walvoord, J. F., R. B. Zuck, and Dallas Theological Seminary, *The Bible knowledge commentary : An exposition of the scriptures* (Wheaton, IL: Victor Books, 1983-c1985), 2:893.
15. Alford, Henry. *New Testament for English Readers*, 1983 Baker Book House, Grand Rapids, Michigan 49506

16 Heritage of Great Evangelical teaching Featuring the best of Martin Luther, John Wesley, Dwight L. Moody, C.H. Spurgeon and others. 1997, c1996 (electronic ed.). Logos Library Systems. Nashville:Thomas Nelson.
17 *The Pursuit of God, The Pursuit of God*, copyright 1948, 1982, 1993, by Zur Ltd. Used by permission of WingSpread Publishers, a division of Zur Ltd. 1.800.884.4571
18 Schaeffer, Francis August. *True Spirituality*. Tyndale House Publishers, Inc., 1971
19 Charles Stanley, *The Glorious Journey*, Stanley, Charles F., Logos Library Systems, *The Glorious Journey* Nashville, TN: Thomas Nelson, 1997, 1996.
20 D. A. Carson, *New Bible Commentary*: 21st century edition (4th ed.). Leicester, England; Downers Grove, Ill., USA: Inter-Varsity Press.
21 Ferguson and Packer, eds., *New dictionary of theology*, Downers Grove, IL: InterVarsity Press, 2000, c1988.
22 Oswald Chambers, *My utmost for His highest, Selections for the Year*. Grand Rapids, MI. Discovery House Publishers, 1993, 1935.
23 Andrew Murray, *Heritage of great evangelical teaching : Featuring the best of Martin Luther, John Wesley, Dwight L. Moody, C.H. Spurgeon and others.* 1997, c1996 (electronic ed.). Nashville: Thomas Nelson.
24 Charles Stanley, Logos Library Systems, *The Glorious Journey* Nashville, TN: Thomas Nelson, 1997, 1996.
25 Charles Stanley, Logos Library Systems, *The Glorious Journey* Nashville, TN: Thomas Nelson, 1997, 1996.
26 Chambers, Oswald. *My Utmost for His Highest: Selections for the Year*. Grand Rapids, MI. Discovery House Publishers, 1993, 1935
27 *Matthew Henry's Commentary on the Whole Bible*, Ruth 2:1–3.
28 *Matthew Henry's Commentary on the Whole Bible: Compl. & Unabridged/One Volume.* Peabody: Hendrickson, 1996, 1991.
29 A.W. Tozer, *The Pursuit of God*, copyright 1948, 1982, 1993, by Zur Ltd. Used by permission of WingSpread Publishers, a division of Zur Ltd. 1.800.884.4571
30 John MacArthur, (*Matthew*) Chicago: Moody Press, 1989.
31 *The Pursuit of God, The Pursuit of God*, copyright 1948, 1982, 1993, by Zur Ltd. Used by permission of WingSpread Publishers, a division of Zur Ltd. 1.800.884.4571
32 Kempis, Thomas à. *The Imitation of Christ*, (1996) Oak Harbor, WA: Logos Research Systems.
33 Richard F. Lovelace, *Dynamics of Spiritual Life* (Downers Grove: IVP, 1979), 49–50.
34 From *Nelson Study Bible: New King James Version, Hazelton's Bible Commentary* (Eerdmans, 1963), and New Bible Dictionary (InterVarsity, 1996).
35 R. F. Youngblood, Nelson's New Illustrated Bible Dictionary : An authoritative one-volume reference work on the Bible with full color illustrations (F. F. Bruce, ed.), electronic edition of the revised *Nelson's Illustrated Bible Dictionary*) (Nashville: Thomas Nelson, 1997).
36 S. G. Hardman and D. L. Moody, *Thoughts for the Quiet Hour* (April 19), Willow Grove, PA: Woodlawn Electronic Publishing, 1998. Originally published by Revell (Chicago), 1990.

www.ingramcontent.com/pod-product-compliance
Lightning Source LLC
LaVergne TN
LVHW011911080426
835508LV00007BA/336